Dancing

WITH
THE

Darkness

MOVING THROUGH POSTNATAL DEPRESSION

Michelle Allan-Ramsay

BALBOA.
PRESS

A DIVISION OF HAY HOUSE

Balboa Press books may be ordered through booksellers or by contacting:

Balboa Press
A Division of Hay House
1663 Liberty Drive
Bloomington, IN 47403
www.balboapress.com.au
1 (877) 407-4847

Print information available on the last page.

ISBN: 978-1-5043-1286-8 (sc)
ISBN: 978-1-5043-1287-5 (e)

Balboa Press rev. date: 07/25/2019

For My Angels
~ Tayah and Kai ~
You are the sparks of my soul
You are the best of me
You are my rock
Because of you I try harder, I question
more, I feel more deeply
You are the Blessings in my life

And For
~ Miles ~
Who stayed, even when the weather was bad
And believed, even when he wasn't sure why
You are a beautiful, strong soul and I am
blest to share this journey with you!

I strive to achieve a life in balance,
a life where the black dog
has no voice.

I strive for freedom.

Contents

Preface

"Life is not about
Waiting for the storm to pass,
It's about learning to
Dance in the rain"

~unknown~

My journey through postnatal depression has seen me learn many things, and the theme of dance has been a strong part of this. For me, dancing has always been a huge part of who I am. I have always danced as a way to process my life, my emotions, my thoughts. But, when I was at the deepest part of my postnatal depression journey, I found I couldn't dance. I couldn't even sway with the music! It was as if my soul had been removed and I sobbed for this loss. I had to force myself to move in any way I could – tapping my fingers, tapping my foot, nodding my head…. anything to start movement in my body. Every movement brought emotional angst because I dance from my heart which was locked away in the darkness. It was a really slow and painful path back to dancing, but I knew it was part of my recovery.

I've become very conscious of how I use language in relation to illness and recovery. During my journey out of postnatal depression, I came across teachers who talked about how we label experiences and how that labelling can become part of our identification process. For example, an experience of postnatal depression, became 'my depression'. But once I start calling it 'my depression' isn't it possible that it then becomes part of how I identify myself, and therefore much harder to let go of? I remember sitting in a café and overhearing a gentleman talking about 'my cancer' and realising how much we do this. Although he sounded very positive, I was intensely struck by how many times he fondly called it 'my cancer' as if it were part of his family. It left me wondering if it becomes harder to overcome an illness that has become part of your identity.

Equally interesting for me, was the use of violent language that I was now becoming aware of. How often do you hear phrases such as 'my fight with cancer', 'the war on drugs', or 'my battle with depression'? Surely, if we are 'fighting' something, we are using force, anger and resistance to try to defeat it? If we focus only on defeating an illness, we may forget to allow healing in.

Becoming aware of my use of language left me in a quandary. If I don't want to personify the depression, but I also don't want to be battling it, how do I talk about it in a way that allows healing? IT exists, and I needed to find a way to relate to it.

The to and fro, back and forth, circling around the language began to feel like a dance. I was dancing between owning depression and fighting it – keeping it close or resisting it fiercely. Sometimes depression and I are partners waltzing together, moving, never keeping still and stuck. At other times, I dance alone in the light, knowing that depression may move out of the shadows and towards me, but never owning me. I know the dance will continue and, at times, we may be close together, at other times far apart, but I also know that the dance is always happening…the darkness isn't permanent.

Dance creates a point of light for me and revives hope. To think of my experience as dancing through the darkness, helps me to remember the darkness isn't me.

Why Did I Write *"Dancing With The Darkness"*?

Postnatal depression is a very lonely illness – as are all mental illnesses. During the years I was ill, I looked everywhere for books that would help me understand what I was going through and find ways to heal. Autobiographical books reassured me that I was not alone in what I was experiencing, however they made my pain more intense, as I identified so strongly with the pain of the writer. Psychological books made me feel even more overwhelmed with the list of things I should be doing to get well. I also had incredible difficulty maintaining enough concentration to be able to comprehend and assimilate so much information.

"Dancing With The Darkness" has been written to help you when you are lost in the 'black cloud', when cognitive function is impaired, when reading is no longer easy because concentration and comprehension are fractured… when all the great books on depression may be just too much information or just 'too many words'. My hope is that *"Dancing With The Darkness"* will inspire, comfort, reassure, and inform. It is not a program, method, or

course to be followed. It does not pretend to have all the answers.

"Dancing With The Darkness" is a book of hope. A collection of wisdom, thoughts, facts and questions meant to provide inspiration and support. It is a friend to turn to in the loneliness of the night. A friend reminding you that you are not alone, that you will get through this, and reminding you to hope. Hope gives us the courage to keep going.

Medical Condition or Something Else?

The classification of postnatal depression belongs to the medical model. It is classified as a Major Depressive Disorder in the Diagnostic and Statistical Manual of Mental Disorders (DSM). However, if we limit our understanding of postnatal depression to a purely medical issue, then we must assume the only path to wellness is via medical intervention – medication and/or psychiatric counselling. And, while these methods have value, is this all there is? In following the medical approach to its logical conclusion, all postnatal depression should be healed via the medical approach. But this isn't so.

Medication doesn't work for everyone. Counselling doesn't work for everyone. Is this because postnatal depression, and maybe other mental health issues, are not simply medical illnesses?

Those who suffer depression often refer to it as 'the dark night of the soul'. Doesn't this infer that the experience is, in fact, a journey of the soul? There is an over-riding sense of darkness during depression. *The black dog, black winds, dark night of the soul* are just some of the terms used to describe depression. The antidote to darkness is light, but how do we get the light in?

I believe there are many paths to the light. The medical approach is to use antidepressants to increase the serotonin in the brain. Cognitive Behaviour Therapy introduces light via logic and reason. Acupuncture increases the light of Qi by rebalancing Yin and Yang energies in our body. Through meditation, one attains a mind of clear light – a connection to the divine.

Is there a more important lesson to be learnt from postnatal depression? In searching for ways to wellness, I encountered a path I had not considered before. A path that led to the Divine, God, Universal Spirit – whatever term you use, it is the universal creative power that resides in each one of us. I wondered if my disconnection from spirit was a major contributor to the postnatal depression.

Further research led me to understand the value of mindfulness practices, the interplay of energy, nutritional requirements, and even quantum theory – how our thoughts create reality.

"Dancing With The Darkness" is my chance to share some of these amazing revelations and how they relate to postnatal depression. *"Dancing With The Darkness"* is not a religious book – it is, however, a book about spirit. The spirit of health.

"Dancing With The Darkness" has been written in the spirit of simplicity. Guided by spirit and experience, I have included succinct pieces of information on a variety of topics to provide comfort and illumination for my readers. Often

I have commented on the information I have quoted as a way to demonstrate its relevance to my healing journey. Sometimes I have left a quote to stand on its own – trusting the clarity of its wisdom. My hope is that you will seek out more information on the topics that resonate with you, for they will be important to *your journey* to wholeness.

I have divided my book into the following sections to assist you to access the information on particular topics in an easy manner.

Introduction – A Journey Through the Darkness

The journey through postnatal depression is a lonely one. Even when you are surrounded by loved ones, the sense of isolation can be enormous. I remember feeling like there were two of 'Me' – the physical 'Me' that people saw, and the real 'Me' inside that was screaming out "Why can't anyone see the pain I'm in?"

There was a constant sense that people really didn't understand what I was going through, which only reinforced my sense of loneliness. Platitudes like "It's just the baby blues", "It'll pass soon" or "Everyone has bad days" just made me realise that others didn't understand the severity of what I felt. Such comments made me feel worse, as they felt like a criticism. I believed that people thought I was weak for 'not coping' with the normal demands of motherhood.

The Introduction is about my journey with postnatal depression. I feel it is important for you to know that the information in this book is based on experience. I hope that if you identify with my experiences, you will be reassured that you too can heal. I hope to inspire you to follow your Spirit to healing.

The Importance of Sleep and Support

If we want to support our children, then we need to feel supported, and support comes in many packages. It can be the offer of help with domestic chores, the giving of a casserole, an ear to listen, a shoulder to cry on, an opportunity to go to a yoga class or movie, or even the chance to sleep without interruption. Although these things may not seem like much, to an over-whelmed mum they are priceless. Sleep deprivation is a tool used to torture people in war because it impairs attention, reasoning and problem solving – skills required by us in caring for our children. It also leads to anxiety and depression.

Nutrition

Beyond merely providing energy for our bodies, nutrition plays an important role in mental health. The neurotransmitters involved in depression (dopamine, noradrenalin, & serotonin) can be adversely affected by nutritional deficiencies. Nutritional supplementation helps the body and brain by providing sufficient levels of essential vitamins, minerals, amino acids and healthy oils. Certain nutrients are also important in maximising our body's ability to utilize any medication we are prescribed.

Anti-Depressants

In January 2010 "Researchers determined that the typical patient, one with mild to moderate depression, gets the same amount of relief from a placebo as from an antidepressant" [1]

Antidepressants have their place, but they are not the only way to deal with postnatal depression. Maybe our society's dependence on 'the quick fix' has resulted in antidepressants being the first or only method offered to help those with depression. I know that I was surprised when I visited a Doctor about the postnatal depression and the only thing suggested was medication. I fully expected a referral to a psychiatrist but not even this was prescribed. Just the medication.

It is not my intention to criticise antidepressants or those who choose to take them, but it is my intention to spark inquiry. Ask questions about what you are being prescribed. Make an informed decision. That is the purpose of this section in the book – to share the information I have come across that has made me question.

Self Awareness

Self awareness is part of the foundation of healing. It involves becoming conscious of your feelings, motives, behaviour, thoughts and desires. You must become aware of how food affects you, how much sleep you are getting and need, how medications affect you, how you respond to other people, and what thoughts you indulge. It is only by becoming aware of yourself that you can consciously choose to change and heal. Awareness of our thoughts is especially important for we cannot solve our problems with the same thinking we used to create those problems. We must become aware of and be able to change our thinking.

Accepting Change

Another foundational aspect of healing is the ability to accept change, and becoming a parent is a huge journey through the dimension of change. Your daily routine changes, your relationships change, your self-image changes, and your children change from baby to toddler to child to adolescent to adult. Change can be exciting and easy, or it may create anxiety and fear. How we attend to change is crucial for without it, we cannot heal.

The Creative Approach to Healing

Expressive Arts Therapy incorporates the use of art to facilitate access to our unconscious realms and includes drawing, painting, sculpture, dance/movement, guided visualisation, sand play, music, guided visualisation, drama, dream work and poetry/writing. Studies show that when used in a therapeutic manner, the arts have a positive effect on people with mental health problems.

Mindfulness

Mindfulness is the practice of placing your awareness on the present – what is happening, how you feel, what you hear and see, etc. The human mind is very distractible, and always jumping from thoughts of the past, to thoughts of the future. But this is very tiring for the mind and contributes to anxiety and stress. By becoming mindful, we learn to be really present in the moment and can appreciate it more. Mindfulness creates space in our thought stream, and it is in this space that we hear our Spirit.

The Spiritual Dimension of Postnatal Depression

Spirituality is the search for meaning. Postnatal depression leaves you feeling devoid of meaning.

One of my reasons for writing *"Dancing With The Darkness"* is to help extricate postnatal depression from the halls of mental illness. By viewing postnatal depression solely as an illness to be beaten, we fail to see the reason for its existence. It exists as a symptom of our need to address issues in our lives. It exists as an opportunity to face these issues and become more than we were before. Maybe postnatal depression is simply Spirit's way of getting our attention. If we pay attention, then we will hear the messages which will fill us with light and meaning.

The Energy Body

We are more than the sum of our parts. Mind-Body-Spirit all interact to create 'Me'. For real healing to take place, we need to attend to all the dimensions of our Being. Our physical body is the vehicle we currently exist in. Our energy body provides an interface between the physical and spiritual, and consists of meridians, chakras and auric fields. I believe that mental health issues have a huge energetic aspect to them, which is why drug therapies are limited in their ability to 'cure' these illnesses. Drugs can reduce symptoms and temporarily hold depression at bay, but seem unable to effect healing. Attending to our energy body can help the healing of our physical body.

Quantum Theory – Thought Creates Reality

What has quantum physics got to do with postnatal depression? EVERYTHING! Quantum physics is complex and beyond my scope to explain in detail here. If you are interested in the science, then I suggest "Breaking the Habit of Being Yourself" by Dr Joe Dispenza is a good starting point. I will also defer to Dr Dispenza to summarise why quantum theory is important to healing. "The quantum model of reality tells us that to change our lives, we must fundamentally change the ways we think, act, and feel. We must change our state of being. Because how we think, feel, and behave is, in essence, our personality, and it is our *personality* that creates our *personal reality*. So, to create a new personal reality, a new life, we must create a new personality."[2] Thought creates reality – so just as our thoughts have contributed to our illness, changing our thoughts can contribute to our health.

How to Use This Book

It is not necessary to read *"Dancing With The Darkness"* from beginning to end, although you can if you wish to. Another way to work with the information is to simply allow the book to open to a page and read. Allowing Spirit to guide you in this way can draw information to you that you may need to hear at this moment.

It is not my intention to tell you that I know the cure for postnatal depression – I don't. My reason for writing this book is to remind you that *YOU* are your best healer. Only you can work through the issues that brought you to this illness. Only you can choose your path to health. *The factors that contributed to the illness are unique to you, just as the path you choose to travel to wellness will be unique to you. There is no single path to illness and, therefore, no single path to health.* You must try to hear your intuition – what do you need to know? What do you need to do? Which therapy/treatment/activity is right for you at this very moment?

My wish is for your health. Take any information which resonates with you and work with it. Ignore anything that doesn't feel right. Learn to listen – to your body, to your heart, to your thoughts, and to your soul. They are your guideposts in the journey towards health. As dark as it is now, the clouds will disappear, and the sun will shine on you again.

Acknowledgements

When I received the call from Spirit to write this book, I had no idea what would be involved. And, I'm sure that if I had known, I wouldn't have even started writing! But it certainly wouldn't exist without the help and support of some very special people.

I am eternally grateful to my children, Tayah and Kai, for choosing me as their Mother. Not only have they walked the dark path with me, but their angelic presence inspires me to strive harder. You remind me every day that Angels live among us.

It is with grateful wonder that I acknowledge my husband Miles. He has shown a strength and wisdom I could only have guessed at in the early years of our relationship. His ability to watch as his wife disappeared in the illness and wait and hope for her return were amazing. Thank you for always trusting me and for believing that I could write this book.

I will be forever thankful to Elisabeth McGrogan for the many hours she spent reading and re-reading my work. Her attention to detail and questioning mind ensured the script made sense. But most importantly, her steadfast belief in me is something I will always treasure. When my ego would start it's self-defeating rant and I would be ready to give up, Elisabeth would remind me of the book's importance. Your spiritual support & friendship were invaluable.

Heartfelt thanks to Georgina Warner – for years of laughter and soul-deep friendship.

Deepest appreciation to Gus MacAnally for always creating a safe healing space.

Heather and Peter Ramsay, I am sincerely thankful to you for always welcoming and supporting me, and for raising such a wonderful son!

A lifetime of gratitude also to my sister Lisa - you have been, and always will be, one of my greatest friends and teachers; and, to my brothers Mark, Craig and Christopher, for being part of the process even though you probably didn't know you were!

Eternal thanks and devotion to my parents, Jean and Malcolm, for giving me a blessed childhood, a strong sense of family and Spirit, and for teaching me about love.

Introduction – A Journey through the Darkness

Motherhood. You know the picture – the sun streams in on the beautiful, contented baby as she smiles at her blissfully happy mother...their world is peaceful and ordered! But what happens when the image doesn't match up? Instead you have a crying baby in pain with reflux, a mother who hasn't managed more than two consecutive hours of sleep in the last month, a toddler who is toilet training, unsorted washing, a house that hasn't been cleaned in weeks, its 1pm and everyone's still in pyjamas...Sounds like chaos... and it is! This is the reality in millions of homes around the world. Yes, motherhood is a divine journey but a journey that passes through dark forests for many women.

I started to realise that I had entered such a dark forest when my second child was about 4 months old. I was trying to organise celebrations for my birthday and finding it arduous. In the past I had enjoyed organising parties and didn't understand why I was becoming angry every time I had to make a decision regarding the details of the event. I had scaled down my original ideas, as I was 'too tired' to be bothered but, when I realised that the thought of being in a group of people terrified me, even though they were family and my closest friends, then I knew something was wrong. Having worked in the mental health field years before, it didn't take me long to realise that I had Postnatal Depression.

Maybe I should have expected that this could happen. After all, there is a history of mental illness in my family and my pregnancy had not been a bed of roses. I always say that I loved being pregnant but it didn't love me! I had endured seven months of morning sickness (more like *24 hours a day/7 days a week sickness!*) which had left me drained of energy. Add to that carpal tunnel syndrome in both wrists (leaving my hands clumsy and painful), separated stomach muscles, weakened lower back (due to lordosis and previous birthing problems), and pre-eclampsia. My entire torso was covered in itchy and sore acne from the pregnancy hormones. The pre-eclampsia left me looking like the 'Michelin Man' – every part of me was swollen – my fingers looked like bananas, my knees and ankles had disappeared under the fluid, my toes looked like tiny sausages – even my nose had spread out like I was permanently flaring my nostrils! There was so much fluid in my legs and feet that I no longer had any flexion and could only shuffle instead of walk. I was reduced to wearing a sarong and my husband's thongs – nothing else fit me!

I also developed chloasma. Chloasma presents as symmetrical brown patches on the cheeks or elsewhere on the face. It is a photosensitivity reaction in women who are pregnant and is also known as *the mask of pregnancy*. Interestingly the chloasma was not restricted to my face and was not patchy – I was completely covered. I looked like I had been sun tanning for weeks!

An interesting condition that appeared in the last month of my pregnancy concerned my voice. It deepened. It deepened so much that my mother couldn't recognise me on the phone – she would think it was one of my brothers! My Obstetrician told me it was due to the hormones and my voice should return to normal after the birth – it took five months to return. Here I was experiencing the most womanly event in my life – pregnancy – and I sounded like a man! So, by the time I delivered my baby not only did I not look like myself, I no longer sounded like me either!

Due to the separation of my stomach muscles and the good sized babies I carried, people assumed I was further along in each pregnancy than I actually was. When I was five months pregnant with my first child, a woman asked me how much longer I had to go. When I replied "four months", she looked aghast and said "I'm sorry". I'm not sure if she was sorry she'd asked or sorry for how much bigger I might get!

Although I attended all my antenatal appointments, the pre-eclampsia was not diagnosed. My blood-pressure was high but within the normal range for pregnancy and my doctor felt the fluid retention was normal. It was only after my mother insisted I ask for a blood test that it was discovered that there was protein in my urine. I was induced two days later – two weeks early.

By the time my beautiful little boy arrived, I was absolutely exhausted – physically and emotionally. In hindsight, maybe it should have occurred to me that I was at risk for postnatal depression. But it just didn't enter my mind. So, I kept going. Kept expecting so much of myself.

My son and I stayed in hospital for four days longer than expected as he had not regained his birth weight.

Although he was a big baby, the medical staff were concerned that he was not gaining weight as he should. This pattern continued after we left hospital and it was a constant worry about why he was not gaining weight. He developed reflux and had difficulty feeding. He would scream intensely to be fed but within a minute or two of starting to feed, he would fall asleep. My husband and I tried everything to keep him awake and feeding – cool face-washers, undressing him so he was cool, tweaking his toes – nothing kept him awake, so he wasn't getting enough to eat. Some feeds would take two hours of feeding him/waking him/feeding him/waking him. I was told he needed to be fed every three hours but it took me an hour or two to do each feed.

I felt useless. I didn't know how to help my baby. Everyone had an opinion. I was keeping a feeding diary, a symptom diary, and naturally a pooh diary! I was averaging four hours sleep a night and they were not consecutive hours. Because I had always been someone who didn't need a lot of sleep, I just expected I could keep going – maybe others did too.

Still no-one saw the writing on the wall.

The problem with postnatal depression is that it creeps up slowly. It's easy to pass off the early signs as related to caring for a newborn – lack of sleep, frustration, lack of control, lack of knowledge, fear and lack of confidence. So, how do you know when it's more than just that? When everyday is a bad day. When all you do is alternate between crying, feeling numb, and exploding with rage. When you hate being alone – but are afraid of people. When you can't do your normal routine tasks like preparing meals or writing a shopping list. When unusual behaviours appear that you never had before – like stuttering. When the days are too long.

That's when it's time to look for help.

My husband is a shift worker who works twelve hour shifts – days and nights. He travels ninety minutes between work and home. Although he took time off for the birth of our son, he had to return to work by the time Kai was four weeks old. As each working day for Miles is fifteen hours long, this only leaves him nine hours at home to eat and sleep. He couldn't afford to be tired with so much driving. This meant I was on my own caring for both the children, day and night for just under five days a week. With Kai's long feeds, a toddler still at home, carpal tunnel causing pain and clumsiness, and my back becoming worse from all the lifting, I was under a fair amount of stress.

Did I recognise the warning signs? No.

This pattern of chaos continued for months but it wasn't until Kai was four months old and I was having difficulty planning my birthday that I realised I had started walking through the darkness. Around this time, I started seeing a Chinese Herbalist to see if I could do anything to increase my milk supply. The stop/start manner of Kai's feeding and the stress I was under had reduced my milk supply and I hoped to be able to feed for longer. It was this Chinese Herbalist who kept telling me that I needed to take time out. She talked with me about how important it is for mothers to take time out to maintain their health. She explained that taking time away from your children is not abandoning them, but rather making sure you are well enough in mind and body to look after them. I don't remember whether it was an awareness of the fragility of my mental state or my desire to keep breastfeeding that made me follow her instructions, but I began to try and find time. Mostly my time-outs centred around grocery shopping! Although a rather mundane activity, it did, in fact, give my mind space to relax a little. Retail therapy for mums?

Although I had worked with people who had depression in the past, I never realised how much it can affect your mind. Even though I'm not currently experiencing postnatal depression, I still have so many gaps in my memory especially of those 4 years. Some of it doesn't worry me, apart from the embarrassment when people are shocked when they tell me of events I have no recollection of. What does upset me is what I don't remember in relation to my children. I feel as if parts of their childhood have been stolen from me. Although I was physically there, my mind wasn't.

Before children (BC!) I had a good memory. Now, it's not only my memories from the postnatal depression period, but even my short-term memory isn't what it used to be. I've had to learn to put strategies in place to compensate for my memory. I always seem to have lists happening – shopping lists, to do lists, packing lists, timetables, even washing lists! I just can't rely on my memory and whilst many people say 'that's just being a busy mum', I know how much my memory has changed.

As I write this, I wonder why I didn't seek treatment as soon as I realised I had postnatal depression. I think that

I never anticipated the severity of this condition. I didn't know it would take me four years to leave the dark forest. I wasn't keen to take medication and have never responded to the 'talk therapies' and I guess I just never thought to attend to it. My back had also become a major problem by this time and took any 'me' attention. By the time my son was one year old, I had been referred to a back surgeon for an opinion. As I had to wait a few months for an appointment with the back surgeon, I decided to see my acupuncturist for help with my back – a very wise decision, as it turns out. During those months, my back improved enough that I cancelled the surgeon's appointment. And, during those months, I realised that not only was my back improving, the acupuncture was helping to lift my moods. I would return from appointments feeling lighter, and a little more able to cope with everyday life.

A few months after starting acupuncture, I read in a health magazine that oestrogen dominance had been linked to depression. As I had a rather 'hormonal history' including poly-cystic ovarian syndrome, I thought this warranted further investigation. I reasoned that if I were oestrogen dominant then appropriate medication may redress that situation and help me recover from the postnatal depression. I discussed this with a doctor who, after appropriate testing, prescribed hormone cream and tablets. Armed with what I thought was an answer, I was optimistic this would help. How could it not? It was tailored to my specific needs. Ten days later I stopped the treatment – I was a complete mess. I had regressed six months and was crying all the time, anxious, overwhelmed and unable to function. When I consulted the doctor, he told me it was not due to the prescription—there must be something else wrong!

A month later I went to see another doctor armed with my previous test results and the prescribed treatment. He felt that one of the hormones I had been prescribed, DHEA (dehydroepiandrosterone) may be part of the problem. DHEA is a steroid hormone that's produced naturally by the adrenal glands. The body converts DHEA into oestrogen and testosterone. He felt that my body may be converting DHEA into oestrogen only, thereby contributing to the oestrogen overload already in my body. So, I tried again – removing the DHEA and reducing the amount I took of the other hormones. Again, I fell into a teary mess and gave up on the hormonal option.

Two months later and I was so tired from the struggle. I was now eighteen months into the illness and starting to fear that maybe it wouldn't end. I alternated between numbness, tears and anger all the time. I had no patience and felt guilty every time I lost my temper with the children. It was as if a monster were inside me and I never knew when it would appear – snarling and spitting venom. My children didn't deserve this behaviour but I was unable to hold the muzzle on this beast. I knew when I began thinking repeatedly that suicide would protect my children from the monster, that it was time to consider my last option – medication. (Note: even though this happened three and a half years ago and I am well now, writing about this time has brought unexpected tears. Such was the intensity of that time. What memories do my children have?)

I spoke to a doctor I trusted about medication and whether something like St John's Wort would suffice. She felt I was too ill for St John's Wort and wrote me out a prescription for Zoloft. I did some research on the internet about this drug. I went to the pharmacy three times to fill the prescription and three times I left empty handed. Even though everyone I spoke to encouraged me to go on the medication, I just couldn't do it. I knew people on this medication and they all said it helped, but still I couldn't do it. I felt as though Spirit was holding my hand to stop me handing the prescription over to be filled. I was desperate and despondent. I didn't understand why I couldn't just take the drugs and be ok. I thought maybe Spirit knew my body would react badly – just like it had with the hormones. But I just wanted the pain to end.

I told my acupuncturist about my struggle with medication. He listened then said "Let's try a change". I didn't know what he meant but I knew the needles always helped. This balance was the turning point in my illness. My acupuncturist also uses Qi Gong and the energy in the room that day was beautiful. I felt so much energy moving through my body it was euphoric! From that balance on, I never thought about taking medication again. I felt the light begin to shine – dimly at first but there was light. Light in my spirit. Light dispelling the darkness.

It confused me that some people were disappointed that I had refused the anti-depressants. But I've never been good at doing things just because people think I should and, in this case, Thank Goodness! If I had taken medication, this book would not have been written because I would not have recognised the spiritual journey that I had started. It would've been like training to climb Mt Everest only to stop at Base Camp and say "OK. That's enough. I'll look at other people's photos from the top of the mountain". What would be the point? There is a deepening of awareness that comes from walking through the darkness – an awareness of self, spirit, humanity and empathy.

And that's the point of it. There is something to be learnt from every illness. Whether it is to understand what triggers your illness, to show you a different way of being in the world, or to remind you of your spirit – there is purpose for its existence. I am a different person now. Some changes are frustrating – like my weak memory, my inability to take on too many projects. But what I have gained is exquisite – my spirit!

"You cannot get to the soul through the intellect".[3] Was postnatal depression the gift that let me lose my grip on the intellect so I could travel the spiritual path? I had faith when I was young but the more I studied, the more I analysed, the more intellectual my faith became. When I was young I believed in the entity of God but through postnatal depression I am learning about being a co-creator with Spirit. As Caroline Myss says we have to give up our idea of a parent-child relationship with God and work beside the God-energy as a co-creator. That is empowering. That is spiritual health.

I believe that my journey through postnatal depression occurred because of a combination of factors – exhausting pregnancy, lack of sleep, feeding difficulties, lack of support, hormonal imbalance. But it primarily occurred because I was disconnected from Spirit. Pregnancy made me feel so very human and fragile. I was locked into a body that was not coping with the changes of pregnancy. I remember a great heaviness and being very focussed on just coping with the exhaustion. I believe that if my spiritual practices had been more developed then I would not have had to experience such a dark night of the soul.

Postnatal depression, or any mental illness, is a multidimensional illness. It doesn't just affect your mind, but your heart, soul and body. As such, the path to health needs to incorporate these aspects. To treat only one element is to miss the lessons of the illness. There is no single path to illness and, therefore, there is no single path to health. Each person needs to evaluate her own history to see what factors contributed to bringing her to this point – diet, sleep, support, mental attitudes, spiritual practices, or something else. Which factors are major issues to be dealt with? What lessons need to be learnt? Which attitudes need to be changed? It is only by understanding what brought you to this illness, that you can start to understand how to manifest the changes that will bring you lasting health.

Conventional thinking on postnatal depression, and depression in general, reasons that stress, and chemical imbalances create these illnesses. But this thinking provides limited options for treatment and, whilst medication and counselling have their place, they seem unable to prevent depression re-occurring. It is only by allowing your Spirit to guide you that you will see the path to long-term health illuminated.

My journey back to health has been a long one. It is not as if everything returned to normal straight after I experienced that wonderful acupuncture balance. That was just the start of my recovery. Acupuncture and Chinese Herbs helped my body and energy become more balanced, counselling helped me work through relationship issues, past-life regression allowed me to see patterns that I had carried for many lifetimes that needed release, meditation helped me gain clarity and contentment, and reading has shown me other ways to think about mental health. I have learnt that it is not just important to talk to Spirit, but it is important to listen. For in listening you hear the song of your soul.

My purpose in writing this book is to remind you of the light. In the absence of the light your soul wilts. It is in your hands to find the way to the light in your soul – only YOU know the way. Just listen.

THE IMPORTANCE OF SLEEP, TIME-OUT, AND SUPPORT

"When a woman gives birth, the process releases enormous energy for renewal and healing. Something deep within her longs to connect with and heal her own family. If her relationship with them is lacking in some way, this healing feeling will be heightened. The contrast between what could be and what actually is can add to a sense of loss or grief that contributes to depression." [4]

Motherhood and sleep deprivation seem to be accepted as being mutually-exclusive – but sleep deprivation is a major contributor to postnatal depression. Just as important, are the issues of time-out and support. One Doctor told me that postnatal depression didn't exist in his country of birth because a new mother was not allowed to do anything but sleep, eat, and feed her baby. Her and her husband's families took care of everything else for the first few months, allowing the woman to recover. This is also true in traditional China where a woman is given support and care during the first forty days following childbirth – a time referred to as the 'Golden Month'. As Xiaolan Zhao says in her book "Traditional Chinese Medicine for Women",

"After Zhao Zhao was born, even if I rested, my family remained. The support they offered by their presence was very important to me and helped me get through those first days, then weeks, with love, care and physical help. Perhaps this family involvement in China is one of the reasons that there is a much lower incidence of post partum depression as compared to the west."[5]

When talking with other women who have had postnatal depression, it has struck me that most of them felt unsupported during their illness, and continue to feel this way after they have recovered. In our society, where being a 'super mum' or 'yummy mummy' is applauded, have we lost the ability to support each other? Why do women feel the need to return to pre-pregnancy bodies as quickly as possible, or to have homes that look more like display houses? Our society of independent, high-achievers seems to have resulted in a society lacking in human caring. Where are the pots of soup? Who's helping to change diapers and do the washing? Who's getting the groceries? Instead of viewing childbirth as a sacred time for connection, and providing support to the women so they can heal, we schedule our visits and keep them short so mothers can rest. But how can they rest when they have to entertain all these 'short visits' and then be *left alone* to soothe a baby disturbed by all the fussing visitors? Maybe we need to learn how to offer or receive help, instead of feeling we are intruding or being needy?

"The nuclear family, where the woman takes the primary role in childcare, is an absolute set up for psychopathology later in life" [6]

"It takes an entire village to bring up a child" (African proverb)

Caroline Myss states that the birth family's purpose is the child's physical well-being. This got me thinking that, if this is true, then maybe the purpose of grandparents/ extended family is to instil wisdom. I find my greatest frustration is how much time the physical requirements of parenting takes – the cooking, cleaning, washing, shopping, etc. I feel these things deprive me of time with my children.

I remember the time I spent with my grandparents and how precious that was to me. We would spend hours looking over recipes, shopping for ingredients, and cooking just one dish! But it wasn't just about the cooking; it was about the bond that was being created. I was learning about patience, the value of listening and being listened to, the wisdom of older generations, and the importance of time.

I watch my children's grandfathers, who both enjoy their gardens, patiently walk around the garden with the children, discussing plants, discovering bugs, watering, raking....just being. These are magic moments that allow the bond to deepen so that my children appreciate the world and other people's opinions. Moments that let the children know they are important enough to be listened to, fun to spend time with, and where they learn that older people have value and wisdom and love to share.

Our society has lost its' community to a great degree. We live such 'independent' lives but at what cost? We have bigger houses than previous generations, but fewer people living in them. Many people live far away from their families. Elderly parents move into retirement villages rather than moving in with their adult children. Many people have left traditional churches and therefore have also left the church community and its support. Maybe the increasing isolation from community impacts on depression by leaving individuals feeling alone and unsupported. The traditional village no longer exists and maybe we need to replace it with a new version. Maybe we need to stop giving each other 'space' and start giving each other support. Maybe we need to learn to ask for and to offer support.

I believe that most people with mental health issues will, at some stage, search the internet for help and information. The internet provides a 'safe' medium – a way to search for information without revealing your pain to others. A medium which allows you to remain anonymous if you wish.

I tried many times to use the internet to find answers but usually came away feeling frustrated by what I found. Most of the easily available information was grounded in medical/psychological jargon, advocating the need for a strong support network of professionals – the local doctor, the psychiatrist/psychologist, the maternal health nurse, etc. It just sounded so overwhelming to me! I could think of nothing worse than a plethora of 'experts' telling me what I needed to do.

What if the GP and the psychiatrist have competing advice? At one stage, I had 2 different Maternal Health Nurses give me opposing advice regarding my first baby's weight gain. One nurse told me that my baby was sleeping too long at night and not eating enough, so I had to wake her at 10pm and feed her. There is nothing like telling a new mum that she's not feeding her child enough to upset her completely! So, I diligently woke my child every night for an extra feed. One month later, I returned to the health centre to be told by a different nurse that I didn't need to do this. My baby's weight gain was fine. The charts the original nurse based her 'advice' on were based on bottle-fed babies, however breast-fed babies gained weight more gradually. Two nurses working in the same office giving out different advice. I had one month of worry, waking my baby every night and for what? It made no difference to my child's growth, but a lot of difference to my peace of mind.

I must say here that I wholeheartedly advocate the need for support for women experiencing postnatal depression. All mothers need a strong support network as parenting is a time of joy, worry, sleeplessness, and a million other emotions. What I also advocate is that the support network should be relevant and nurturing. All women deserve to feel that their concerns for their baby are heard, that they know their baby better than anyone, that non-judgmental advice will be given, and support offered, not imposed. A support network may consist of a medical practitioner, a homeopath, a sister, a parent, a friend, a mother's group, a priest, a spiritual teacher - anyone that loves and supports you. A support person listens to you, suggests, helps you find your own answers, and accepts your choices.

Serotonin is the feel-good brain chemical that has been found to be depleted in the brains of those with depression. It is formed in the brain during the REM sleep cycle, and if your REM cycle is interrupted, you won't create enough serotonin. Many of the anti-depressant drugs prescribed for depression increase the amount of available serotonin in the blood stream. However, according to NINDS (National Institute of Neurological Disorders and Stroke), many antidepressants suppress REM sleep. This seems to me to be a little like pedalling forward and backward on a bicycle at the same time. We need REM sleep to make serotonin, but if we take antidepressants to increase our serotonin, we actually may suppress REM sleep, thereby reducing the serotonin our body makes.

"During sleep, we usually pass through five phases of sleep: stages 1, 2, 3, 4, and REM (rapid eye movement) sleep. These stages progress in a cycle from stage 1 to REM sleep, then the cycle starts over again with stage 1... The first REM sleep period usually occurs about 70-90 minutes after we fall asleep. A complete sleep cycle takes 90 to 110 minutes on average. The first sleep cycles each night contain relatively short REM periods and long periods of deep sleep. As the night progresses, REM sleep periods increase in length while deep sleep decreases. By morning, people spend nearly all their sleep time in stages 1, 2, and REM." [7]

Most mothers are sleep-deprived. That's a fact! And, from my own experience, in the early months of my baby's life, I was averaging 4 to 5 hours sleep over the entire night, with the longest sleep period being 1 hour. So, if the complete sleep cycle takes 90 to 100 minutes, and the first REM period starts after about 70 to 90 minutes, and I was hardly ever getting 60 minutes sleep at a time, I guess I hardly ever reached REM sleep in those first months. Without REM sleep my body's serotonin manufacturing would be impaired, contributing to postnatal depression.

NUTRITION

"..when we're deficient in one micronutrient – selenium, zinc, or any vitamin - it makes it difficult for us to make optimal use even of those nutrients that are present in adequate quantities, compromising even more the integrity of our response to stress, the health of our brain, and quality of our mood. Finally, when we're under stress, as we are when we're depressed, our need for nutrients tends to increase." [8] Good quality supplements can make a huge difference to your mental health. It makes sense to see an integrative doctor or naturopath who can advise you about which supplements will help and which brands are most effective. Not all vitamins are created equal!

"The brain has a high requirement for B vitamins (especially B6) and is unable to manufacture adequate amounts of the neurotransmitters serotonin and dopamine without them. These neurotransmitters control mental energy, concentration, memory and sleep patterns. Deficiencies of the B group vitamins can lead to depressive symptoms and dysfunction of the spinal cord and nerves."[9]

Supplements can assist anti-depressants to be more effective by ensuring their uptake by the brain.

"Fish oil confers another unique benefit most people don't know about. It helps re-establish and expand the 'roadway' that the serotonin has to travel over. The SSRIs (Selective Serotonin Reuptake Inhibitors) cause more serotonin to circulate in the blood stream. But the feel good chemical can't get to the brain without this 'roadway'. ..Individuals have enough serotonin just no way to get it where it's most needed."[10]

NB. SSRI's are the most commonly prescribed type of antidepressant.

"Magnesium is a mineral that is required in greater amounts in those with stress and anxiety. This is because magnesium exerts a calming effect upon the central nervous system and helps nerves and muscles to relax. When we are stressed our bodies use up far greater quantities of magnesium, and magnesium deficient people overreact to minor stress." [11]

An easy way to get magnesium is by soaking in an Epsom bath. The Epsom will be absorbed through your skin helping ease muscle aches and pains, as well calming your nerves.

"Insufficient intake of water can have many adverse health effects and when it comes to your brain, hydration is vital as around 75% of the brain consists of water. Depressed people often consume a lot of coffee or caffeine containing sweet drinks such as soft drinks. These beverages can be dehydrating and will not take the place of water. Dehydrated brain cells do not perform their functions well and lack of water also makes the blood thicker, reducing the circulation to the brain. Try to drink at least 8 glasses of water daily and ideally around 2 litres of water daily will optimise brain function. Herbal tea can be classed as water but don't use too much sugar as then it becomes dehydrating.... Increasing your water intake not only improves mental energy and moods but also reduces aches and pains and headaches."[12]

Dr Cabot, in her book "Help for Depression and Anxiety" discusses nutritional aspects of these illnesses and gives practical advice on dietary and nutritional supplementation to support mental health. As she writes "..use of natural therapies along with a brain boosting diet will allow smaller doses of antidepressant drugs to be much more effective." [13] Here is some of the information that struck a chord with me.

"Mineral deficiencies can lead to impaired production of the brain's neurotransmitters. The mineral magnesium, along with vitamin B6, is required for the conversion of the amino acid tryptophan, into the happy chemical serotonin."[14]

Depressive illness is often associated with low levels of serotonin in the brain. Whether these low levels of serotonin are the cause or result of depression still seems to be open to discussion – conclusive research has not yet been demonstrated.

"L-Tryptophan is converted into the neurotransmitter serotonin in the nervous system and if adequate amounts of tryptophan are not present in the diet, a deficiency of serotonin can occur. This can result in depression, anxiety and insomnia."[15] Dr Cabot provides a list of food sources of tryptophan in her book as it is an essential amino acid, meaning it must be obtained from the diet or supplements.

"Depression and anxiety can be greatly aggravated if the diet does not provide adequate amounts of the essential fatty acids. The most important fatty acids for the brain are the omega 3 fatty acids known as EPA and DHA.... Studies have shown that in depressed subjects who have a poor diet, devoid or very low in omega 3 fatty acids, a remarkable improvement in mental and emotional health is achieved by giving supplements of fish oil. Scans of the brains of these depressed subjects showed that the size of the brain increased after giving the fish oil supplements and especially the areas of the brain concerned with emotion and memory." [16]

"Vitamin D is made from cholesterol in the skin. When the sun's ultraviolet B (UVB) rays penetrate the exposed skin the cholesterol is turned into vitamin D. Vitamin D is required for a healthy nervous system and a healthy immune system."[17]

Dr Cabot has found that over 50% of her clients are vitamin D deficient, even those living in sunny climates. This is due to factors such as sunscreens, hats and long hours working indoors. She suggests exposing more skin to sunshine (avoiding midday sun and sunburn) and vitamin D supplementation if your levels are low, and your mental health may improve.

Excess weight gain and cravings can often be experienced by women with postnatal depression. Dr Marcelle Pick discusses how one of the issues affecting weight gain can be a neurotransmitter imbalance. What interests me, is that these are the same neurotransmitters that are involved in depression, such as serotonin.

When you are depressed, your body is in an almost constant state of fight-or-flight. In this state, your body releases the hormone cortisol, which Dr Pick says is the major hormone responsible for a neurotransmitter imbalance. This surge of cortisol, results in corresponding surges in serotonin and insulin, followed by a drop in both a few hours later. Low serotonin results in carbohydrate cravings.

"Carbohydrates are your body's main source of glucose – brain fuel. They are readily broken down, and they provide a relatively quick source of energy and an increase in serotonin, the body's feel good neurotransmitter. The problem with carbohydrates today is that most of us get them from the wrong source – from refined grains and sugar, instead of whole grains, fruit and vegetables. Eating refined sugar and grains causes a huge spike in glucose and insulin followed by a precipitous blood-sugar and serotonin crash that triggers a craving for another hit." [18]

"Reduce inflammation. Inflammation is one of the key factors in depression, and studies show that mothers with PPD (post partum depression) have higher levels of inflammation.....Anxiety in first-time mothers, for example, is strongly linked with activation of the inflammatory response. So anything you can do to decrease anxiety and inflammation in your body is a good first step toward treating or avoiding PPD naturally.....One good approach is to discontinue the use of foods that are known causes of inflammation, such as refined sugar or flour, caffeine, and alcohol. At the same time, you can increase your intake of nature's best anxiety-dissolvers and anti-inflammatories, such as omega-3 fatty acids and safe, gentle herbs (good for moms and babies) such as turmeric, boswellia and motherwort.

Exercise, cognitive therapy, and the herbal antidepressant St. John's Wort have also been shown to help down-regulate inflammation. You have many choices, but for best results, consult with a professional, particularly if you're breastfeeding—there are some herbs that are not necessarily good for your baby, and should be avoided until you wean your baby." [19]

ANTI-DEPRESSANTS

Anti-depressants are frequently prescribed for women with postnatal depression and many women find these to be helpful. I don't wish to tell anyone that they should or should not take anti-depressants – this is a very personal decision. However, I wish to share some of the information I have found during my research in order that people are able to make informed decisions about their health care.

The following is taken from an article written by Dr Christiane Northrup who is a pioneer in the field of the mind-body-spirit approach to women's health.

"In 2008, we learned that the benefits of antidepressants had been greatly overstated. Former FDA psychiatrist Erick H. Turner, M.D. uncovered some startling information about Selective Serotonin Reuptake Inhibitors (SSRI's), including Prozac, Paxil, and Zoloft, the most commonly prescribed antidepressants. In reviewing all the medical literature, he learned that 94 percent of the reports showing the therapeutic benefits of SSRIs were published compared to only 14 percent of the reports showing either no benefits or inconclusive results (of taking SSRIs). When he weighed all the literature, Dr. Turner determined that SSRIs were no more effective than a placebo for treating most depressive patients. Those with severe depression were helped, sometimes greatly, but those with mild to moderate depression, the majority of cases, received little relief. British researchers, using the Freedom of Information Act, uncovered identical findings.

In January 2010, another study published in the Journal of the American Medical Association (JAMA) confirms these findings. The newest study also evaluated another class of antidepressants, tricyclics antidepressants. Again, researchers determined that the typical patient, one with mild to moderate depression, gets the same amount of relief from a placebo as from an antidepressant." [20]

Dr James S. Gordon is critical of the use of antidepressant medication and also of the evidence upon which their prescription is based. However, he is quick to point out that if you are convinced by what he has to say, and you are currently using antidepressants, *you should not just stop taking them.* The drug withdrawal symptoms are potentially dangerous and you should go off them slowly and under medical supervision.

According to Dr Gordon,

"..there is no good evidence that depression – whether major depressive disorder or dysthymia – is a disease in the way that insulin-dependent diabetes is. There are no consistent pathological post-mortem findings in the brains of those who are depressed. The genetic association, though present, is hardly overwhelming, and the studies that describe it are significantly more problematic than most accounts indicate. Meanwhile, a fifty-year research effort has turned up no consistent biochemical abnormalities in the brains, spinal fluid, or blood of depressed people.

Though some studies do show an association between low levels of serotonin and depression, there is still no proof that most people with low levels of serotonin or other neurotransmitters..are depressed, nor have most depressed people been demonstrated to have low levels. Nor is it clear whether any such altered level of neurotransmitters might be the cause, or the consequence, of depression, or what relationship it might actually have to depression. Indeed, recent research strongly suggests that stress and the action of stress hormones are more likely causes of depression and of observed changes in neurotransmitter levels. In any case, no tests are used in clinical practice to pinpoint either those who do have lower levels of neurotransmitters or which substance might be lower or, indeed, who might best respond to which antidepressant." [21]

The placebo effect represents our positive ability to influence our biology. "Doctors should not dismiss the power of the mind as something inferior to the power of chemicals and the scalpel. They should let go of their conviction that the body and its parts are essentially stupid and that we need outside intervention to maintain our health." [22]

Funnily enough, mainstream medicine tends to regard the effect of the placebo is 'all in the mind', which quantum science is actually proving to be true. Dr Bruce Lipton calls it the *belief* effect rather than the placebo effect!

"A Baylor School of Medicine study, published in 2002 in the *New England Journal of Medicine* evaluated surgery for patients with severe, debilitating knee pain. (Moseley, et al, 2002) The lead author of the study, Dr. Bruce Moseley, 'knew' that knee surgery helped his patients: "all good surgeons know there is no placebo effect in surgery." But Moseley was trying to figure out which part of the surgery was giving his patients relief. The patients in the study were divided into three groups. Moseley shaved the damaged cartilage in the knee of one group. For another group, he flushed out the knee joint, removing material thought to be causing the inflammatory effect. Both of these constitute standard treatment for arthritic knees. The third group got "fake" surgery. The patient was sedated, Moseley made three standard incisions and then talked and acted just as he would have during a real surgery – he even splashed salt water to simulate the sound of the knee-washing procedure. After forty minutes, Moseley sewed up the incisions as if he had done the surgery. All three groups were prescribed the same postoperative care, which included an exercise program.

The results were shocking! Yes, the groups who received surgery, as expected, improved. But the placebo group improved just as much as the other two groups... (Dr Moseley wrote) "My skill as a surgeon had no benefit on these patients. The entire benefit of surgery for osteoarthritis of the knee was the placebo effect." " [23] The placebo patients didn't find out for two years that they had received fake surgery. One of the placebo patients, who walked with a cane before the surgery, was able to play basketball with his grandchildren after surgery.

The placebo effect has also been shown in studies to be a powerful treatment for depression and other diseases. "In a 2002 article in the American Psychological Association's *Prevention & Treatment*, "The Emperor's New Drugs," University of Connecticut psychology professor Irving Kirsch found that eighty percent of the effect of antidepressants, as measured in clinical trials, could be attributed to the placebo effect."[24]

SELF-AWARENESS

For many women, Postnatal depression is a single episode that, once gone, never returns. For others, like myself, it is the start of a life-long journey. Once I considered I had recovered from postnatal depression, I thought it was plain sailing from then on. Within a year of recovery, I realised I was wrong. During the illness, one of the 'ticks' that I experienced was a stammer. It wasn't a full-blown stammer but I would get stuck repeating words and have to stop talking to stop the stammer. That 'tick' is now one of my warning signs. If I find myself getting stuck on words and repeating them over and over, then I know I need to attend to my stress levels. I know that if I don't deal with whatever is causing me stress, then the depression may reoccur. Postnatal depression has taught me that I need to remain aware and learn new coping skills—skills that are making me a more conscious and balanced person.

Naming the beast

Does it matter whether you acknowledge that you have depression or not? Having worked in the mental health industry, amongst so many 'normal' people who happened to have mental illness, I didn't feel any stigma about saying I had postnatal depression. In fact, it was more of a problem for other people around me! I have always felt that by talking about it and identifying that I had it, then it normalised the illness. Sometimes I would mention it as a way of explaining why I was not acting in my normal fashion!

Many people are uncertain about identifying that they have depression – even to themselves. Maybe they fear that naming it makes it real, or that by naming it they will succumb to it more.

Maybe they fear that others will look at them differently once it is identified.

Does it really matter whether you say 'I have postnatal depression' or not? The label of postnatal depression is not the real issue here. The real question is, are you dealing with the darkness in your head and heart? It doesn't matter what it's name is, it matters what you do with it. It matters that you can identify that something important is happening and requires your love and attention.

It matters that you are listening to your heart and body. You feel the uncomfortable quiver in your stomach at the thought of everyday activities. You feel the dizzy sensation in your head when you are trying to organise an event. You notice the strange new 'ticks' or behaviours that have appeared in response to stress. You hear the change in your language as particular words appear more regularly – words like 'overwhelmed', 'stressed', 'can't'.

Be careful what you read and who you turn to for advice. There are many people with good intentions and good opinions but that doesn't mean they are right for *you*. Trust your intuition. If an opinion loads you up with guilt then maybe it's not relevant to you. I found that I had to abandon all the traditional and popular parenting books as they simply contributed to the guilt that seemed inherent in parenting. I have a funny cartoon in my head that has a new mother leaving hospital. As the medical staff hand her baby to her, they say 'Here's your beautiful new baby and your free bag of parental guilt'!

As silly as this sounds, I think most mums would agree that guilt just bubbles up once you have a child. If your baby cries a lot, you are bombarded with questions like – is it reflux, is it hunger, is it pain? If I just cuddle my baby am I creating a dependency later in life like the books say? Can I cuddle my baby too long? Should baby sleep alone or in my room/bed? Cloth vs disposable nappies? Breast vs bottle? Your baby has a rash – what have YOU been eating. And don't even get me started on the vaccination issue!

Whilst most opinions are well-intentioned, a new mother can be fragile after a long birth and sleepless nights. Opinions need to be offered in a gentle manner rather than delivered as a final judgement.

And how do you withstand the barrage of medical opinions? From nurses who have been working in midwifery so long that they just KNOW how everything happens, to well-dressed specialists who must know everything because we pay them such huge amounts of money. Maybe we'd get more relevant information if people were paid for results, not opinions!

As Dr. Christiane Northrup says "Embedded in the medical model..is a victim mentality"[25]. It is this victim mentality that keeps the guilt piling up. We need to take control of our health and our baby's health and filter all information given to us. When my son had reflux, I kept trying all the different strategies and medications that the paediatrician advised, but nothing helped. In desperation I wondered what else I could do and phoned my Chinese Herbalist to ask if she could work with such a young baby. She gave me a herbal remedy to give my son and the improvement was immediate. When I told my paediatrician that I was using Chinese herbs, he asked me what the ingredients were and warned me to be careful as I didn't know what was in the preparation. I suggested that I didn't know what the ingredients were in his prescriptions either! I didn't get much response to that.

It is crucial to find teachings, practises, advice and techniques that support you in your parenting role. Inspiration to guide and support you rather than admonishments for tasks you haven't done.

It is very easy to get caught up in the 'perfect parenting phenomenon'. At some point society seems to have decided that we had to become 'Yummy Mummies', 'Domestic Goddesses', successful career women or business owners, Perfect Parents, and Sexy Mummas.

WHY?

Where is the reality in all this? Driven by our insecurities and extreme tiredness, we are sucked in by the images of celebrity mums who return to pre-baby bodies 4 weeks after birth. We forget the fact that they all have personal trainers, nannies, cooks, money and agents to make it easy.

Images of perfect homes pervade advertising, subconsciously telling us that this is how all homes should look. Even advertisements for shower cleaning products don't really have dirty showers!

A pervading attitude in modern parenting is that if we don't get everything right then our children will be scarred for life.

I've noticed that even children's shows contribute to the perfect parenting phenomenon. Homes in these shows are always tidy, fathers always happy and playful, and mothers always have huge amounts of time to play with the children, cook and look lovely. Angelina Ballerina's mother is always happily cooking in the kitchen – peaceful and serene. Peppa Pig's parents both work but have time every day to roll in muddy puddles and laugh! So are our children being programmed to expect perfect parents too?

We have to remain conscious all the time of the thinking we are being exposed to. If being with certain people or groups leaves you feeling 'inadequate' in any way, then maybe you should review why? Are you buying into a group attitude that is out of sync with your thinking? Are you amongst very competitive people when you are not a competitive person yourself? Is the subconscious agenda of the group a desire to prove who is doing the best?

Always check in with how you feel. If you feel energized by those you spend time with then this will translate into your parenting and health. If you feel drained by those you talk with, then maybe their attitudes or energy are not in line with your own. Surround yourself with positive and supportive people, and only expose yourself and your children to literature and TV shows that inspire you all. Rely on your own intuition rather than seeking out information from books, magazines, or TV shows.

Your children are a reflection of you.

When you are stressed – they will feel stressed and act accordingly. When they are stressed, you will feel more stress. Which will usually make their stress worse, and your stress worse, and so on! And so the cycle continues.

If your baby is crying and you are becoming stressed about how to help him, then he will feel your stress and respond to it more. I don't say this as an accusation. I'm not saying you are the reason for your child's distress. I say this in order to help you understand that you can help your baby even when you don't know what is wrong. Remaining calm and trusting that you are doing all that you can will allow you to soothe him even when you don't know what is wrong. Sometimes there is nothing you can do but hold and rub and soothe your baby – with love.

Babies are so sensitive to the energy around them, and they are especially sensitive to their parent's energy. I really saw this in action during my illness. Although I knew meditation helped, I struggled to maintain concentration for any length of time. What I would do, however, is go to sleep with a meditation CD playing. I joke that I was trying to become 'subliminally enlightened'! What I quickly discovered, however, was that when I fell asleep with my meditation playing, I would awake the next morning in a slightly calmer state than on the days when I had not played the CD's the night before. The meditation CD obviously helped my emotional state even though I was not actively meditating.

Now, on those mornings when I was calmer, my baby woke up calmer and happier than on the days where I was feeling low and helpless. When I had not played my CD, my baby was a grumpy mess the next morning. Why? Because when my energy was calm, my baby felt that and was free to feel happy. However, when my depression was intense, my baby just felt the pain and cried. The interesting thing was that my baby's reaction to me was not based on how I greeted him, on him actually seeing my mood. I could hear his emotional state through the baby monitor. So, his happy or stressed moods reflected mine without him actually being in the same room as me. That's how important our energy fields are – they are bigger than us. And, as such, we need to be aware of them and learn to work with them responsibly.

I have heard stress referred to as the silent killer because most people don't recognise when they are stressed. Long term stress can lead to depression, so it is a good idea to recognize some of the signs of stress, including:

- Shallow breathing
- Tightness in the body
- Tension in the jaw
- Headaches
- A rise in blood pressure
- Chest pain
- Feeling overwhelmed
- Inability to concentrate

If we learn to recognise the signs of stress sooner, we can implement strategies to alleviate our response to it and prevent stress escalating into depression. Pema Chödrön discusses different strategies that can help us when we feel that familiar tension. One of these is simply to stay present. You can practice staying present by pausing and taking three deep breaths. Another way is to simply sit and listen. Listen to the sounds close to you, then listen to the sounds further away. No judgement, just listening.

Pema also talks about 'dropping the storyline', which I have found to be a huge factor in my response to events. "It's the conversations we have with ourselves in that neutral moment when we acknowledge we're hooked that turn a slight feeling of unease, a vague tightening of our jaw or stomach, into unkind words, dismissive gestures, or even violence. But it will remain an ember and gradually die out, the energy will ebb and then it will naturally flow on, if we don't fuel it, if we don't freeze it, with our storylines."[26]

I can turn an uneasy feeling into a full-blown issue about being a social leper, and no-one liking me, and what a failure…..in 5 seconds. All I need is that storyline to anchor the pain. Or, I can breathe deeply, look up at the clouds and not allow the storyline to develop.

Many of our perceptions, and misperceptions, were programmed during our early years. Beliefs like "I'm not wanted", "I'm stupid", or "I don't deserve good things" are downloaded into the subconscious and replayed throughout our lives.

According to Dr Lipton [27], this is due to the level of brain activity we exist in as children. When brain waves are measured using an EEG (electroencephalograph) machine, adults display the complete range of activity – high, low, and everything in-between.

Newborn babies and children up to two years of age, start out in the lowest level of activity – Delta. Adults are asleep or unconscious when in this state.

Children from 2 years to 7 years old are predominantly in the next level – Theta. This is the state of imagination and creation where a child mixes the real world with their fantasy world. Adults experience this state when drifting into and out of sleep – when the real and dream worlds can become confused.

By age 7, the child moves into Alpha activity – a state of heightened consciousness and activity. By 12, the child moves into Beta activity which is a more focussed school-room type of consciousness.

The relevance of this is that for the first 6 years of a child's life, there is a predominance of delta and theta activity – those levels also associated with hypnosis. So, it appears the child is in an hypnotic trance for the first 6 years of its life. In this hypnotic state, the child doesn't need to be actively taught as it learns by watching and experience – everything will be downloaded. Perceptions of the world are downloaded directly into the subconscious. It's here where we acquire our perceptions of life and here where we acquire our mis-perceptions of life.

The subconscious mind is more powerful than the conscious mind and runs our behaviour from 95-99 per cent of the time. Over the past thirty to forty years, people have been going into therapy to try and reveal all the painful and hurtful things that have happened to them, believing that once they consciously knew where the pain came from they would change their subconscious behaviour. The problem is "that the subconscious mind doesn't have anybody in it – it's a tape player!" [28] Just talking to the tape player doesn't change what it is playing. We have to change what is recorded on the tape player by changing our perceptions.

"Illness is not the problem. *You* are the problem – as long as the egoic mind is in control. When you are ill or disabled, do not feel that you have failed in some way, do not feel guilty. Do not blame life for treating you unfairly, but do not blame yourself either. All that is resistance. If you have a major illness, use it for enlightenment. Anything 'bad' that happens in your life – use it for enlightenment. Withdraw time from the illness. Do not give it any past or future. Let it force you into intense present-moment awareness – and see what happens.

Become an alchemist. Transmute base metal into gold, suffering into consciousness, disaster into enlightenment.

Are you seriously ill and feeling angry now about what I have just said? Then that is a clear sign that the illness has become part of your sense of self and that you are now protecting your identity – as well as protecting the illness. The condition that is labelled "illness" has nothing to do with who you truly are." [29]

How do we change the perceptions we hold?

> Listen to the thoughts you are thinking. Most of our thoughts are redundant, repetitive or negative. Pay attention to them and change them. If you constantly reframe your thoughts to be positive and abundant, then over time you can rewrite them. This is what the Buddhists call Mindfulness. If you stop replaying the past, or worrying about the future, then you can train your thoughts to remain in the present. Postnatal depression was my spirit's way of stopping my untrained and negative thought patterns. It's as if my obsessive and negative thought patterns became amplified in the early stage of the depression – more thinking, more worrying, more analysing – until there came a time when I could think no more. My mind came crashing down – I had overloaded the hard drive! I had to retrain my mind to focus, comprehend, and act. I had to learn to watch my thoughts and not dwell on repetitive and negative thought patterns, instead learning to reframe negative thoughts into positive ones.

> Clinical hypnosis is effective according to Dr Lipton [30] as it puts us into the same state we were in when we were originally programmed – Theta brain activity.

> Energy psychology. Dr Lipton says there are many modalities that deal with reprogramming the energy field and allow for super-learning. Some of the modalities he mentions are PYSCH-K, EFT (Emotional Freedom Technique), EMDR (Eye Movement Desensitization & Reprocessing), and BODYTALK.

I remember those long nights spent breastfeeding my baby. Night after night I would sit there with my mood changing from peaceful to annoyed to impatient. Interestingly, these difficult emotions seemed to occur mainly on the nights my husband, Miles, was home. Now, you may be thinking that we must've been arguing or something similar on the nights he was home. But no, he was just sleeping.

He is a shift-worker who works twelve hour days and spends 3 hours travelling. With such a physically demanding work routine, it is important that he gets as much rest as possible. I have no problem with that. So why was I always annoyed when he was home? Because he was sleeping and I wasn't, and that's all I could think about.

I would get up to feed my baby during the night without an issue. It's a beautiful calm time of the day and I could feed him without any other issues pressing on my attention. Or could I?

Initially we would start each feed sitting peacefully in the dim light. My son was a slow drinker and an average feed took one and a half hours. After a while, the mental chatter would start...I wonder if he is nearly finished, how do I stay awake when I'm so tired, how long have I been awake, how much sleep have I had so far tonight, I'm sure Miles gets more sleep than me even accounting for the shift work, blah blah blah.

And there it was! My mind went searching for issues and found them, and then the stress set in. The annoyance, the irritation, the overwhelm, the feeling that I was all alone.

After months of counting how much sleep I was getting and how much sleep Miles was getting and comparing how much worse off I was.... I just got sick of it. I realised that the more I focussed on who was wearier, the more stressed I got, and nothing was changing. So, I stopped counting minutes of sleep. I stopped looking at the clock when I got up during the night, so I couldn't count how long I was up for. Amazingly, I started feeling less tired because I wasn't focussing on how tired I was. I was still sleep-deprived, but it didn't feel so much like the world was out to get me! My son still took a long time to feed, but I was ok with that now. I didn't get stressed about it. The change in my perception and energy meant that my son no longer had to deal with my emotional charge and could feed in peace! We could now enjoy this time together.

Our perceptions are so distorted during depression. In the depressive state, I thought I was just *mulling* things over to work problematic situations out and would become annoyed that those around me displayed signs of disinterest after a time. I thought they were being very rude and unsupportive. I now see how repetitive my thinking was at that time. No wonder people got bored at hearing the same thing over, and over, and over, and over again! I now see this behaviour in others – the continual churning over and over of life's events.

Depression makes us behave differently and, in turn, our behaviours can feed our depression. If we continually run the negative mental programs of "I'm a bad mother", "I'm so stupid" and "what did I say that for?" then we are less likely to pursue those things that give us pleasure. The less pleasure we experience, the more negative our thoughts become. A fleeting thought of failure can trigger a huge sense of fatigue.

"When a negative thought or image arises in the mind, there will be a sense of contraction, tightening or bracing in the body somewhere. It may be a frown, a stomach churning, a pallor in the skin or a tension in the lower back." [31] This is the body's preparation to fight, freeze or run – the fight-or-flight reaction. This means that most of our blood is being sent to our extremities to facilitate running or fighting, and less blood is being directed to the internal organs, including the brain. We become less intelligent and therefore have difficulty choosing positive thoughts and behaviours. So it is important to try and intercept our negative thoughts before they happen and replace them with positive affirmations that support our growth.

"When there is no way out, there is still always a way *through*. So don't turn away from the pain. Face it. Feel it fully. *Feel* it – don't think about it! Express it if necessary, but don't create a script in your mind around it. Give all your attention to the feeling, not to the person, event, or situation that seems to have caused it. Don't let the mind use the pain to create a victim identity for yourself out of it. Feeling sorry for yourself and telling others your story will keep you stuck in suffering. Since it is impossible to get away from the feeling, the only possibility of change is to move into it; otherwise, nothing will shift. So give your complete attention to what you feel, and refrain from mentally labelling it. As you go into the feeling, be intensely alert. At first, it may seem like a dark and terrifying place, and when the urge to turn away from it comes, observe it but don't act on it. Keep putting your attention on the pain, keep feeling the grief, the fear, the dread, the loneliness, whatever it is. Stay alert, stay present – present with your whole Being, with every cell of your body. As you do so, you are bringing a light into this darkness. This is the flame of your consciousness." [32]

What is the ego?

"Ego is the unobserved mind that runs your life when you are not present as the witnessing consciousness, the watcher. The ego perceives itself as a separate fragment in a hostile universe, with no real inner connection to any other being, surrounded by other egos which it either sees as a potential threat or which it will attempt to use for its own ends." [33]

"We are all connected to people, places, things, traditions, beliefs, habits, and ideas. To some degree, we tend to define ourselves by these connections. For example: I'm Frank's daughter and Maryanne's best friend; I live in a Connecticut suburb; I love chocolate, the colour purple and yellow Labrador retrievers…" [34] Buddhism and other philosophies regard these things as attachments. These attachments cause us suffering because we are too focused on them and fail to pay attention to the present moment. We identify so strongly with our attachments – our ego identity – that we miss the truth of the present moment. Ego is the source of the delusion that we are disconnected from the Divine.

"When we are driven and motivated by our habitual likes and dislikes, we are tossed about by karmic winds that blow us uncontrollably in all sorts of directions without leaving us much chance to choose or navigate." [35] It is by learning to live in the present moment – the Now – that we create our chance to consciously navigate through our lives.

When we live with present-moment awareness, we become aware of our 'attachments' and how they cloud the view of our true self. It is this mindfulness that allows us to make choices about our behaviour and thinking rather than simply (over)reacting to events we experience.

That is the power of Now.

ACCEPTING CHANGE

ACCEPTING CHANGE

Motherhood is a series of 'letting go' experiences.

During pregnancy and the early months of parenthood, a mother may need to let go or accept changes to:

> Her career
> Her health
> Her body image
> Her freedom

During her child's life, she will experience letting go of

> Her newborn – who is now an infant
> Her infant – who is now a toddler
> Her toddler – who is now a young child
> Her young child – who is now an older child
> Her older child – who is now a teenager
> Her teenager – who is now an adult

Each transition brings with it the joy of seeing your child grow and experience life, and the sadness of knowing the infant/toddler/child/teenager stage has passed forever. That is a parent's journey and it is important to acknowledge each transition, allow yourself to grieve if necessary, and move forward with joy and acceptance.

"Unhappiness itself is not the problem – it is an inherent and unavoidable part of being alive. Rather, it's the harshly negative views of ourselves that can be switched on by unhappy moods that entangle us."[36] Acknowledging that our thoughts are what get us stuck, allows us to look at changing our reactions.

"The hardest thing about change is not making the same choices as you did the day before." [37]

Dr Joe Dispenza suggests that intention is the start of making change. Start by asking yourself 'what is my intention' and then write it down. Research on changing habits shows that when you write down your intention, you have an 80% chance of reaching your goals. Writing it down tells your brain that you mean it.

Once you have written down your intention, write down a list of what he calls 'sponsoring thoughts'. Sponsoring thoughts are the reasons why you want this intention and are the driving force to get you there.

Then, track your changes – through journaling, a spreadsheet, a whiteboard on the wall – whatever way helps you to see your success. Research shows that when you begin to change one habit, it's easier to change others.

Dispenza suggests cueing your environment to support you. Place pictures, words, quotes that remind you and inspire you towards your goals.

"When you get your behaviour to match your intentions, and your actions equal to your thoughts, then you get your mind and body working together. Now you are mastering exactly what you set out to do, and now when you begin to experience the effects of your choices, those new experiences then begin to reaffirm the emotion that you created from your sponsoring thoughts. Now the loop is starting to change and your choices begin to become a new habit." [38]

Although our society is heavily geared toward education these days, we are actually not taught how to think, how to learn, how to communicate, or how to respond to an ever-changing world. And whilst we may survive in the world and even think we are successful, becoming a parent can quickly undo all that. I always say I was a fabulous parent...until I had children! Parenting brings out all our insecurities and fears. It exposes our heart so that 'reasoned' decisions become so difficult. No matter how educated we are or how much we want to 'do it better' than the previous generation, we may unconsciously repeat the parenting we received. Why?

Is it because we have never been taught to review our behaviour, so in the busy-ness of parenting we fall back on what we learnt as children? Parenting is an incredibly emotional experience. A wise parent doesn't 'know it all' but knows they have more to learn. Never look at learning as an expression of failure, but as an acknowledgement of greater wisdom to come. Learning is not just about facts like feeding formulas, developmental milestones, or how to cook nutritious baby food. Learning is about trusting your maternal instinct, facing your fears with courage, understanding new parenting strategies, learning mindful parenting, and so many other beautiful and insightful dimensions.

"The journey through and beyond depression requires a balance of action and acceptance. Sometimes, the emphasis has to be on action that moves you forward – finding and choosing a physician or Guide, buying and preparing mood-healthy foods, creating lists to help you respond to the Call (to change). Other times, action precedes relaxation and acceptance. You have to set aside the time to meditate or actively create the images that can reduce your stress or guide your choices. Then you need to relax into the experience, to accept the guidance that comes." [39]

"We start to feel bad, and before we know it we've been pulled down into the spiral, and no amount of struggle will get us out. In fact, the more we struggle, the deeper we end up mired." [40]

Lessons of the spirit have their own timeframe. To struggle with depression is like trying to hold back the storm winds. Release your need to fight. Change your attitude from one who is fighting or giving up, to one who bends with the black winds, just as the trees bend in the wind. Allow the pain to move through you and it will leave. Allow the lessons to surface without frantically looking for them. Wisdom comes when it does.

"Surrender isn't the same as submission. Submission means giving up, resigning yourself to the limitations that are holding you back or keeping you down. In surrendering, you're opening yourself up to the current of your life, which is always moving, always changing. And you're inviting and embracing the deep changes that are starting to work inside of you." [41]

The transformation of emotions
is not about
'getting rid' of or 'trying to change'
the emotions.
Rather, it involves seeing them
so clearly and deeply
that we cease to do unskilful things
with them and around them.
This is how change begins. [42]

"Whatever life takes away from you,

let it go.

When you surrender

and let go of the past,

you allow yourself to be

fully alive in the moment." [43]

Letting go of the 'ideals' of my pregnancy.

It took me a long time to accept that having an epidural during my first child's birth was ok. I had committed to a natural birth and had no reason to believe it was not possible for me. A chiropractor had told me years before that I had a wide birth canal and so giving birth would be easy for me. The nurse running the ante-natal class said she thought I would birth easily because I was so relaxed and positive. I had my bag packed with massage oils, meditation music, and other things that would help create a wonderful birth experience. I wasn't going to lie down, but would have an active birth – maybe even a joyous birth!

Oh yeah? Think again...

39 hours of labour, failure to progress, so much pain that I was blacking out all the time, and the gas they gave me for pain relief did absolutely nothing. Finally the doctor advised that I needed to have an epidural and hormones to bring on the birth, as my baby's heart beat was showing signs of tiring. After two epidural injections and a couple of hours, I finally had my beautiful angel in my arms!

After we left the hospital, however, I started to punish myself for having been too weak. I thought I had given in too easily and now my baby had been subjected to an unnatural birth experience and drugs. Had I damaged her in any way? Was I weak? What went wrong?

It took me a while to accept that without such intervention, my daughter and I would probably have died. I heard of another woman and her baby who had the same difficulties I had but she had refused medical intervention. The woman and her child both died. I realised how lucky I was to have accepted the help that was suggested.

It's funny, but part of my letting go of my 'ideal' birthing experience was to understand that it was my inability to 'let go' of my baby that caused the long birth. I realised that whilst I was pregnant, my baby and I shared a sacred space together – a bond so precious it defies words. Whilst I was looking forward to holding my baby in my arms, I was terrified to let her out into the world. It was the end of a sacred time. And while she was inside me I felt I could protect her but once she was in the world, I had to share that responsibility with others. I had to trust others with this precious little soul. I guess I just didn't trust the world enough.

"If we cling to unreality, we lose our sanity." [44]

There can be a lot of 'unreality' in motherhood....the perfect pregnancy, an easy birth, a baby that eats and sleeps on cue from day one, always knowing what to do as a mother, a perfect house with all duties complete, a quick return to a pre-baby body, blah, blah, blah

I'm not saying these are not possible, but to expect all of this 'perfection' is unrealistic and sets us up to fail. Surrounded by marketing, TV shows, social media, and books that tout the beauty and ease of parenting, it can be easy to feel inadequate when you are still in your pyjamas with dishes in the sink and a crying baby at 3pm in the afternoon.

And if we think that our lives will be the same as they were before, with the addition of the perfect baby, then the reality of sleepless nights, fussy feeding, unsettled baby and all the other changes, will surely pave the way to insanity...unless we accept the changes, good and bad.

Your life has changed, and it is imperfectly perfect!

It is no accident you are reading this book.

It is no accident you are here at this moment.

The universe will give you everything you need.

Open yourself to everything.

Surrender to the process and

everyone and everything you need will appear

at just the right time.

Accept that change is inevitable

and brings with it many blessings

Trust it is as it should be.

"The practice of letting go asks a lot of us. On an external level, think about all the things that we don't want to relinquish. Think about possessions, money, youth, people, accomplishments, career, and status. On an internal level, notice how we cling to self-concepts and images, to our ideas, opinions, beliefs, politics, and habitual ways of doing things; think about how attached we are to our feelings, moods, regrets, grudges, memories, and the stories we tell ourselves. Think about all the ways we try to hold on to and control all the aspects of our lives." [45]

I never thought of myself as a control freak, in fact I thought my lack of boundaries, hatred of routine, and time mismanagement were symbols of absence of control. But, yet another lesson I am learning from motherhood is about my need for control.

But, maybe it's not so much 'control' as 'power'. Not power over others, but power within myself. I've been feeling like the ball in a pin-ball machine – repeatedly hit this way and that by the flippers – having no control about what happens in my life.

The 'flippers' for me include:

- Managing our time to get to school 'on time'
- After school activities
- My husband's shift work
- Meal planning
- Shopping
- My work hours and their unpredictability
- Cleaning especially when my husband sleeps during the day
- Establishing good homework routines for the children
- Bedtimes

It feels as if there is no 'ME' in all of that – it's all about everyone else. Well, that's what I thought!

I realise that because the depression makes me feel out of control within myself, I have developed a strong urge to control the different elements in my life that buffet me around. The problem with this is that when situations don't go as I plan them, then I 'lose the plot'.

For example, the children's bedtime. I would set a time that I felt was good for the children to allow plenty of sleep. Night after night we would run late and it didn't seem to matter how I changed our nightly routine, I just couldn't get the children to bed on time. Every night as the clock ticked closer and closer to the 'deadline,' I would get panicky. I would start focussing on what a bad mother I was because now the children wouldn't get enough sleep, on how pathetic I was that I couldn't organise our lives to meet this time frame, and then I would get angry and my beautiful children now had a grumpy mum to tuck them in.

I had to realise and accept that this just wasn't working. The more I tried to control things, the worse things got. I decided it was more important to enjoy my life rather than control it. The real power lies not in controlling the details of my life, but in changing my perception of those details. What was more important—the children being put to bed on time by a grumpy mum or getting put to bed a few minutes late by a happy mum? Once I asked myself this question, the answer was easy. And funnily enough, when I stopped stressing about bed times, we actually started to get to bed on time! Go figure!

HEALING AND CURING

"I believe that people have the ability to self-heal and that once they understand their capacity to do so, they will move to fulfil their potential for wellness. I think it's important to distinguish healing from curing. I see healing as the process of becoming whole and finding meaning in our circumstances. It involves harmonizing all aspects of ourselves – physical, emotional, mental and spiritual. The Chinese word that refers to all these levels is *xin*, meaning 'heart-mind'...

Curing is generally focused on eliminating or reducing symptoms or disease...Treatment is focused on stopping, controlling or removing a specific condition...Healing helps us to connect to who we are within a 'larger' context, whatever we understand this to be. It brings our inner sense of solitariness into relationship with something 'greater' than ourselves. We are in synch, in harmony, with ourselves and our environments. Even if curing is not possible, healing can still occur...

Health is not merely the absence of disease; it's about living in harmony with all levels of ourselves, *xin*, and recognizing that this is a changing and dynamic state of being." [46]

THE CREATIVE
APPROACH TO HEALING

Dr James Gordon, in his book 'Unstuck: Your Guide to the Seven-Stage Journey out of Depression', promotes the need for movement as an important part of disrupting the pattern of depression – both in our bodies and minds.

"Depression...is a kind of stuckness, in body as well as mind, a fixed pattern of feeling, thinking and being. Depressed people...feel burdened physically as well as emotionally, palpably constrained by forces that seem beyond them. Disrupting this fixed pattern – in body as well as mind and spirit – helps make change possible. In fact, working with the body is the most powerful, direct, and reliable route to surrender, change, and freedom." [47]

"exercise – movement – alters brain chemistry and with it mood." [48]

"thirty to forty minutes of daily exercise – jogging, biking, swimming, lifting weights, using the StairMaster or treadmill, or walking – reliably raises the levels of serotonin and norepinephrine, the two neurotransmitters that most antidepressants aim at increasing, as well as the endorphins, the brain's pain-reducing and pleasure–enhancing amino acid peptides. Exercise likely increases the number and activity of neurons in the hippocampus that are depleted in depression and seem to be so important to emotional well-being." [49]

"In study after study, exercise..decreases people's depression scores, sometimes by as much as 50 percent, a result fully as good as that obtained by psychotherapy or chemical antidepressants." [50]

Dr Gordon promotes the use of the creative arts as processes to help people move through depression and become more grounded and whole. This is what he has to say.

"Art therapy is a mental health profession that uses the creative art process to improve the emotional, physical, and mental well-being of individuals. Through artistic self-expression, art therapists help clients to reduce stress, manage behaviour, and increase self –awareness. Art therapists use the visual arts (drawing, sculpting, painting, etc) and the creative process, as well as counselling and psychotherapy, to treat anxiety, depression, trauma and loss, addiction, and many other social and emotional difficulties." [51]

"Dance therapy is the psychotherapeutic use of movement as a process to improve cognitive, social, behavioural, physical, and emotional conditions. It is an expressive therapy based on the realization of the mind-body continuum, in which the body's movement may have a positive effect on mental well-being." [52]

"Music therapy is an established clinical and evidence-based health care profession that utilizes singing, creating, moving to and /or listening to music as forms of communication, self-expression, and self-discovery." [53]

During the illness, I felt like I was curled in a psychological ball – holding on for dear life in the centre of a cyclone. I hoped that if I could hold my thoughts still, freeze them in some way, then the torture they were inflicting would cease. That mental 'holding on' translated into a physical holding pattern – my movements became controlled and minimal. Whilst this may not sound like such a problem, for me it was like prison. I did classical ballet/contemporary dance for 16 years, studied dance at university, and have always danced in one form another. Movement is how I express myself. My mother-in-law once commented on the fact I was dancing whilst cooking and asked me what I was dancing to when she couldn't even hear any music. I was dancing to the background music used in a TV advertisement!

At some point during my illness, I realised I was not dancing. I remembered that I had always used dance to help me process and purge any emotional/psychological pain I was experiencing. I thought it strange that I had not thought of this healing option before. So, I put some music on at home one day to dance.....and couldn't. I couldn't move. I just stood there feeling a huge wave of anxiety and grief wash over me. I couldn't dance. I couldn't even move – my breath was taken away. I cried for the loss of my expression. Dance should've healed me as it had before, but I couldn't move. I was too fragile, both physically and emotionally. Dance was my breath – when I stopped breathing deeply as a way to control my mental pain – I stopped moving too. This compounded the illness. Now I need to be brave to dance – to feel again and trust that I'm safe.

Dance is my *vehicle* for letting in the light. What's your vehicle? Dance, art, sculpture, writing, music, craft, drama, painting, model making, gardening, bushwalking, swimming? Everyone needs an expressive outlet. Something that makes their heart sing. Something that feeds their soul. Often, as parents, we become so overwhelmed by the duties and responsibilities we now have, that we 're-prioritise'. Our race cars get sold, our dance classes get cancelled, our art supplies become used for the children's development, and our passions are re-classified as 'optional extras'. But the truth is they are not 'optional' – they are essential to maintaining our sense of 'self'. These 'optional extras' can help us make sense of our internal world and work through our issues – consciously and unconsciously.

"Expressive Arts Therapy works directly with the symbolic world of the psyche, bringing that which lies in the unconscious realm into waking consciousness. In this manner, artistic processes shed light upon and reflect those aspects of the self that lie hidden. This acknowledgment and expression allows for a deeper connection and exploration, and leads to a gradual integration of all aspects of self."[54] When the physical light is depleted by stress, birth, parenting demands, then the spiritual light is needed to heal your soul.

MINDFULNESS

Be present.

This moment is all you have.

For in this moment you are whole.

The activity of the mind is what separates you from spirit. Motherhood can make the mind VERY busy – planning, watching, anticipating, doing – never just being present. Aren't the best times of motherhood spent with your children – just watching them sleep or play, smiling together, experiencing their joy at a new discovery?

This is NOW.

Babies are still connected to spirit without mind activity – this is why they make us so joyful.

To look into a baby's eyes is to look into Spirit. It is Pure Love.

"Mindfulness is our ability to be aware of what is going on both inside us and around us. It is the continuous awareness of our bodies, emotions, and thoughts... Mindfulness helps us to come back to the here and now, to be aware of what is going on in the present moment, and to be in touch with the wonders of life."[55]

Reflecting back, I realise that I created so much stress for myself by not remaining in the moment. When I was sitting feeding my baby and enjoying the feel of his hand clasping my finger, or watching him happily drinking, or playing with him, then I was peaceful. But as soon as I remembered 'the practicalities' of life, then I would feel the panic surge and drown once again in 'overwhelm'.

What do I mean by 'the practicalities'? Things like—is this feed taking too long? Why does he feed so slowly? Is there a problem? If this feed takes 2 hours (he was a slow eater), and he is meant to be fed every 3 hours, then when do I feed him next? Do I let him sleep through a feed time because we spent so long on the last feed? But if I do that, then he will miss a feed and he hasn't been putting on enough weight. If I spend 2 hours at a time feeding him, how will I spend time with my older child, do the washing, get the dinner made.....

I still have the tendency to let 'the practicalities' take over, but I'm trying to practice mindfulness. When I feel the panic start in the pit of my stomach, I take a deep breath to centre me, and talk to myself. I ask myself questions like...although the dinner has to be made; will another 5 minutes spent talking with my child really delay dinner that much? Surely, 5 minutes of quality time with my child will benefit her more than a dinner that is served 5 minutes earlier.

"Happiness is an emotion and emotions fluctuate all the time depending on situations and how you view them...... Cease rating your life by how often you feel the emotion of happiness and embrace all of life's events, including the unenjoyable ones. Instead of thinking these times are an interruption to your happy life, practise finding the value in these events and you will start to feel happier."[56]

This too shall pass.

In the darkest nights, when my fears were the loudest, I would focus on the fact that morning would come soon.

When I would stand looking in the pantry, trying to work out what to cook and feeling the panic rise at my inability to figure out dinner...I would think 'In 2 hours dinner will be over with and this panic will be gone'.

When the anxiety of a social engagement was increasing...I would tell myself that 'by this time tomorrow it will be over'.

When all I could think about was how my suicide would free my family from the pain I was causing....I would remind myself that this illness would pass... but my children's pain at my suicide would not.

This too shall pass.

"As mothers, we often find it hard to relax around our children, never knowing what the next moment will bring: a mess? a demand? a mood swing? danger? To be calmer we must learn to let go of some of our attachment to stability, control and order, and accept that our conditions constantly change. With equanimity we stop battling our way through life and begin to take it as it comes, to roll with the punches."[57]

'...battling our way through life'.... Why do we look at life and its events as battles? Why do we 'battle cancer' or 'battle depression' or 'battle addiction' or any other of the myriad battles humans refer to? I used to refer to my illness as 'my battle with postnatal depression' until one day it hit me...why am I battling?

It can be very interesting to look up the definition of words we use so easily.

| *Battle* | -noun | - a *sustained* fight between opposing forces |
| | -verb | - *fight or struggle* tenaciously to achieve or *resist* something |

I realised that the more I battled my illness, the greater its hold on me. The more intensely I fought against the blackness, the more it resisted me. I could not <u>fight</u> my way through depression or <u>force</u> my brain to work better, or <u>resist</u> the anxiety when it arose. I had to allow it to move <u>through</u> me. That was the secret. The more I pushed myself to be well, the greater the depression felt. I had to stop and accept the changes in me – how my brain now processed information, how many events I could handle in a day, what triggered my anxiety. You can't fight an illness. Illness is your body's way of getting your attention. So, give it your attention – listen to what it has to say.

Battling illness is simply our way of trying to feel in control of the situation. Humans are action-oriented control freaks! We need to think we are *doing* something to overcome the illness. But the more attached we are to winning the battle, the harder it will be to 'win'. We win by learning what has brought us to this place. We win by letting go of our attachment to control and action, and allowing ourselves to hear the whisper of Spirit.

"For most people, acceptance is rarely a goal. Change is the goal, along with achievement and success. Acceptance, in fact, is often equated with failure – failure to succeed, failure to improve, and failure to transcend one's old self.

But acceptance is not the same as failure. ...it implies an overall trust that things are 'good enough'. It also implies tolerance and the ability to respond non-judgementally to others or toward ourselves. Thus, when we face a problem, the first step, before changing it, is to watch it. We simply allow the problem to exist for the moment, and in that moment we become more aware of what the problem is. ..Acceptance and mindfulness...go hand in hand."[58]

I think that what Newberg and Waldman are referring to here is our current society's overriding drive to succeed. But this success seems to be measured in the amount of money we have, how many bedrooms our house has, how high our children's grades are, and so on. For many people today, acceptance seems to imply failure. The implication is that the act of accepting a situation is really the act of giving up – but this is not the correct use of the word.

As Newberg and Waldman say, acceptance is not the same as failure. *Acceptance* – is the willingness to tolerate a difficult situation, whilst *Failure* is a lack of success or effort. Failure gives up, whereas acceptance keeps going.

"Failure views reality (postnatal depression) as no good, a bad thing and a negative state of being. Acceptance views reality (postnatal depression) as an individual human experience, an opportunity to learn from and is a gentle (and positive) reminder that change is possible when we choose to be 'mindul'."[59]

I think this attitude of acceptance is an important step toward healing. By allowing the illness to exist (acceptance), we will become more aware of what the problem is (mindfulness), and hence, we will be able to see what needs addressing in order to heal. This is not failure.

When we have expectations, we become single-focussed – waiting for that expectation to be fulfilled. But if we suspend expectation, we are free to see the gift, guidance, path that Spirit is showing us.

Maybe our expectations get in the way of our parenting. If I expect my baby to feed in 20 minutes, then I will be stressed out by the time we get to 40 minutes. If I expect my baby to sleep for 2 hours every afternoon, then his 30 minute sleep will throw me in a spin. If I expect to always have a solution every time she cries, then I will feel like an inadequate mother. By suspending expectation we are better able to stay present in the moment, and that is when we are more likely to hear the guidance we need. A mother's instinct is strong but it is hard to hear it when our mind is busy telling us that we are failing. Expectation set us up to feel failure.

Suspend expectation and allow yourself to be present in this moment, for then you will see with greater clarity what it is you need to do....or not do.

Whilst I was sick, I knew that meditation would help me but I just couldn't maintain concentration. Then I came across the Buddhist practice of mindful breathing.

Mindful breathing asks that you simply breathe normally whilst counting. However, your mind must maintain focus only on the number you are at – nothing else. So as you count *one*, that is what you focus on. As you count *two*, that is what you focus on, and so on. If you count *two* but think about what to cook for dinner, then start counting at *one* again. The aim is to increase your ability to maintain focus, which is what meditation is.

Well, I couldn't even count to *one* without losing focus when I first tried to do this! That made me giggle. With practice and patience I gradually increased my counting! This was a great technique for me as it gave my excessively busy mind something to do. Asking my mind to 'empty all thoughts' or to just '*BE*', were concepts still too far from reality at the time.

"Simply put, conscious mothering is mothering with an increasing awareness of our unconscious beliefs and behaviours, especially those beliefs and behaviours that are not useful or effective as we raise our (children). We must be careful, however, that we don't take on this practice of increasing our awareness as a burden, as one more thing we have to add to our to-do list in the already-overwhelming role of mothering...Instead, increasing our awareness of how and when to use our intuition will make this task easier, because it will improve communication... Conscious mothering is not perfect mothering. It is a daily practice that does not consider perfection a desirable or obtainable goal." [60]

The Buddhist nun, Pema Chödrön, also talks about increasing our awareness of our unconscious beliefs and behaviours as a way to free ourselves from their sting. In

Buddhist terms they are called *shenpa* – those things that hook us, which create emotional responses, that cause us to tense up and want to withdraw. "That tight feeling has the power to hook us into self-denigration, blame, anger, jealousy and other emotions which lead to words and actions that end up poisoning us." [61]

Acknowledging our shenpa should not be an opportunity to focus on how bad we are for having them, but rather an opportunity to delight in the wisdom we have to *see* the shenpa. Pema gently reminds us not to use shenpa practise as another whip to be used against ourselves. Instead delight in the fact that you can see your shenpa, for if you couldn't see them then you couldn't change them. Buddhist teachings should be a source of delight; not a list of things you don't do.

"Don't believe everything you think...

Thoughts are like stories we tell ourselves all the time. But they're not all true, wise, skilful or helpful. So don't believe everything you think! Ask yourself; is this a helpful or skilful thought? If not, there are various things you can do to diffuse its energy. For example, you can say hello to it, thank it for its opinion and let it go...with a deep exhalation. Or another approach I read about this morning...you can replay the thought, singing it to a silly tune. Try it! It really helps you to not 'believe' the unhelpful story your thought is telling you... ♥" [62]

"Everyone knows what it feels like to be in a situation or environment that is so stressful that it's almost impossible to 'think straight'. That's when mindfulness comes in handy. Even when everything in our lives is going wrong, mindfulness helps us be calm and clear. It keeps us from being overcome and overwhelmed by all those oceanic waves of emotionality and confusion..." [63]

Do not pursue the past.

Do not lose yourself in the future.

The past no longer is.

The future has not yet come.

Looking deeply at life as it is

in the very here and now,

The practitioner dwells

in stability and freedom.

We must be diligent today.

To wait until tomorrow is too late.

~ BUDDHA ~[64]

"As soon as you honour the present moment, all unhappiness and struggle dissolve, and life begins to flow with joy and ease. When you act out of present-moment awareness, whatever you do becomes imbued with a sense of quality, care and love – even the most simple action." [65]

Whilst I am by no means an experienced practitioner of mindfulness, I have found the truth of the above statements. For example, I used to complain about having to make school lunches because I am not great with food planning and organisation. I knew I had to prepare them at night because mornings are always so busy and it meant one less thing to worry about in the school-preparation rush. However, I found it difficult because I was tired and wanting to relax a little before bed. In this mind-frame, preparing those school lunches seemed to take FOREVER!

Now, I try to stay in the present moment and not place my attention on the time it is taking me to prepare the lunches. Just this simple act of ignoring time and staying present in the activity means that I don't notice how long it takes, or how tired my body is. Suddenly the lunches are ready and my 'down-time' is here! It has amazed me how powerful the practise of mindfulness is!

When my mind is busy working things out, trying to synthesize information and generally being too active, I find that solutions and ideas elude me. When I am forced to 'take a break' from my mental gymnastics, either through social engagements, other more urgent activities, or mental exhaustion, then the solution usually finds me. The more I struggle to figure situations out, the less success I have. When a space is created in my mind, the solution appears in the gap!

"Present-moment awareness creates a gap not only in the stream of mind but also in the past-future continuum. Nothing truly new and creative can come into this world except through that gap, that clear space of infinite possibility." [66]

Mindfulness teaches us to be present.

Parenthood is an overwhelming time of schedules, chores, and learning but if that is what we focus on, then that is all we see. The magic lies in not missing the beauty in our child as we rush through our duties. Focus on the miracles – the peaceful breath of your sleeping baby, the tiny socks on the washing line, the complete trust your baby has in you.

At a Metro Station in Washington D.C., on a cold January morning in 2007, a man with a violin played masterpieces that have endured for centuries - Bach, Schubert, Ponce, and Massenet. He played for about 45 minutes. During that time, approximately 2,000 people went through the station, most of them on their way to work.

After about 3 minutes, a middle-aged man noticed that there was a musician playing. His gait changed momentarily as he turned his head to look, then kept walking.

About 3 minutes later, the violinist received his first dollar. A woman threw money in the case and, without stopping, continued to walk.

At 6 minutes, a young man leaned against the wall to listen to him, then looked at his watch and started to walk again.

At one point, a 3-year old boy tried to stop, but his hurried mother propelled him toward the door. The child continued turning his head to look at the musician. This scene was repeated by every child and parent who walked past.

For 45 minutes, the musician played continuously. Only 7 people stopped and listened for a short while. About 27 gave money but continued to walk at their normal pace. The man collected a total of $32. When he finished playing there was silence. No one noticed and no one applauded. There was no recognition at all.

No one knew this, but the violinist was Joshua Bell, one of the greatest musicians in the world. He played one of the most intricate pieces ever written, with a violin worth $3.5 million dollars. Two days before, Joshua Bell played to a sold-out theatre in Boston where the 'not so bad' seats averaged $100 each.

Joshua Bell, playing incognito in the D.C. Metro Station, was organized by the Washington Post as part of a social experiment about context, perception and priorities. The experiment raised several questions. In a common-place environment, at an inappropriate hour, do we perceive beauty? If so, do we stop to appreciate it?

If we do <u>not</u> have a moment to stop and listen to one of the best musicians in the world, playing some of the finest music ever written, with one of the most beautiful instruments ever made . . . How many other things are we missing as we rush through life?

Considering the children were the only demographic who consistently tried to stop and listen, maybe we should take our queues from them about what is important or beautiful?

"When you are full of problems, there is no room for anything new to enter; no room for a solution. So whenever you can, make some room, create some space, so that you find the life underneath your life situation.

Use your senses fully. Be where you are. Look around. Just look, don't interpret. See the light, shapes, colours, textures. Be aware of the silent presence of each thing. Be aware of the space that allows everything to be. Listen to the sounds; don't judge them. Listen to the silence underneath the sounds. Touch something—anything—and feel and acknowledge its Being. Observe the rhythm of your breathing; feel the air flowing in and out, feel the life energy inside your body. Allow everything to be, within and without. Allow the "isness" of all things. Move deeply into the Now." [67]

THE SPIRITUAL DIMENSION
OF POSTNATAL DEPRESSION

The feeling of isolation – the eternal companion of postnatal depression.

Is postnatal depression actually a result of spiritual isolation? Is the rise in mental health disorders in our society actually a reflection of the decline in individual spiritual nurturing? As our lives become busier and more technically oriented, are we relegating our spiritual needs to the back seat? With the rise in disillusionment regarding traditional religions, have we 'thrown the baby out with the bath water' by treating religion and spirituality as mutually exclusive and discarding both?

The world is undergoing massive change in how it relates to religion and spirituality. Many people see the traditional religions as perpetuating hypocrisy – preaching love through pain and atrocity. Their reaction has been to abandon religion and, often, their spirituality in the process. But humans need spiritual connection and relevance, and need to learn a new way of relating to spirit. Maybe mental illnesses, such as postnatal depression, are partially a spiritual madness which leaves us feeling isolated from Spirit.

Do we need to nurture our connection to Spirit / Divine / God in order to regain our spiritual sanity?

"The common ingredient in every single dysfunction is an issue of power."[68]

Depression is an issue of power – a feeling of the loss of power. The power to feed your baby well, the power to help your baby sleep, the power to know why your baby cries so much, the power to get household chores done, the power to sleep. You feel as if 'You', who once had the power in your life, are now powerless to the demands of motherhood. And you feel alone with your powerlessness, as everyone else seems to have control of their lives – except you. You feel powerless to resist the black winds... or so it seems.

This loss of power is not actually real but a symptom of your loss of spirit. When we focus solely on all the thoughts in our head as a busy mum, then we distance ourselves from Spirit and can no longer feel its guidance. We become further locked in our thoughts and lose sight of the light. This is the blackness (absence of light) of depression. The further removed from Spirit (Light) we feel, the deeper our depression and the 'darker' our individual world is. Our thoughts and worries race faster and faster until, inevitably, they crash and we are left in the silence of an exhausted mind.

How do we rebuild our connection to Spirit?

Listen...

Don't force yourself to regain your mind skills of concentration, memory, speech, etc. Just listen. For in listening you will hear your Spirit. Its voice may be quiet but if you have patience and listen, you will hear it. The more attention you give to its voice, the easier you will hear it. Listen – for it will guide you back to health. It will guide you to the therapies, practices, and rituals you need to regain your spiritual power.

We are all connected in the world wide web of Spirit. We all have spiritual power. Once you know this, you will be well. For it is the Light of Spirit that dispels the darkness of depression.

Be gentle with yourself.

You are not the person you were before. Spirit has forced you to stop for a reason. Healing requires that you be gentle with yourself and allow yourself the time to heal.

You do not have this illness because you are in some way defective. You are not a bad person.

This illness has a purpose – to teach you something, to give you wisdom and compassion, to create change in your life.

Pregnancy and childbirth – divine, cosmic
experience or basic human process?

Does the journey of bringing a child into this world, reveal
our innermost belief about this? Whilst I experienced
glimpses of the cosmic magic of pregnancy, my body
became grounded by pain, illness and dysfunction. I felt
betrayed by my body and guilty that I had not manifested a
more divine birth experience for my children and myself.
I felt trapped in the 'humanness' of it all. But, how could
I expect the experience of childbirth to be divine when I
was disconnected from Spirit? Maybe, if my connection to
Spirit had been strong, I would have been able to survive
the humanness of pregnancy and enjoy its divinity.

Doreen Virtue, in her book 'Divine Guidance. How to Have a Dialogue with God and Your Guardian Angels', talks about the true you and the false you. The true you is aligned with, and receives guidance from Spirit. The false you is governed by fear, and is also known as the ego.

Fear was my constant companion whilst I was ill. I was afraid to be alone, afraid to be with people, afraid my children weren't getting enough attention, afraid to make decisions, and on and on. Is depression, therefore, simply a journey into the pure state of the ego? Ego which fears everything and guides you based on these fears.

Ms Virtue suggests that because the false you is controlled by fear, it's guidance is false and misleading, and results in wasted money, energy and time. WOW how true for me! During my illness I spent so much time at the shops because every purchase required two trips. I couldn't make decisions on what I needed, so I would buy a few options, take them home, finally decide on one and then have to return the others. I would waste so much time trying to make simple decisions that I never got all my shopping done at once and would have to return time and time again to complete my errands. Each trip to the shops saw me purchasing things I didn't need – things that my ego urged me to purchase in the hope of filling the emptiness inside. So much wasted time, money and energy!

Any addiction, whether it is a shopping addiction, alcohol, food, drugs, gambling, TV, computer, attitudes etc is the ego's way of distracting you from your pain. But avoiding pain doesn't make it go away.

The ego is not our true self, it is the image we identify with via labels, titles, judgements, and projections. We can only move beyond our ego through self-awareness. As we become aware of our thoughts, our speech, our behaviour, and our patterns, we are able to choose a new path aligned with Spirit.

So, through awareness we move beyond the ego (pain) to the true self and towards God/Spirit.

Pregnancy is the only time when two souls occupy the same space. If we are all really part of the cosmic soul stream, then pregnancy is the purest physical reminder of how this feels. For a brief moment in time, I was joined with my babies. Birth, therefore, left me with separation grief. Grief at being separated from the pure spirits of my babies, and the painful knowledge that my body would not cope with another pregnancy. This was it. The last time I could experience the blissful co-existence. It left me feeling truly alone in my body.

In our culture today, we try our hardest to avoid pain. We deny its existence, pop a pill to erase it, keep ourselves busy so as to ignore it – all the while failing to heed its message. We regard pain as an inconvenience or a punishment for wrongdoing when it is actually a messenger. *Pain appears when we need to address an issue – in our body, our diet, our ways of handling stress, our lifestyle, and even in our spiritual lives.*

If we learn to stop and listen to pain, we will hear the message. If, however, we continue to try and avoid feeling the pain, then the message may need to be transmitted in a louder way i.e. greater pain. As Caroline Myss says, "God stops your life so he can step in it" [69] and I think the level of pain required to stop your life is related to how great your powers of ignorance are. I believe my postnatal depression was so long and difficult because I just wasn't hearing the messages before that. I had become an 'intellectual spiritualist' – all the books and courses I had devoured had not touched my soul, only my mind. But as Myss says "You cannot get to the soul through the intellect."[70] Basically Spirit had to '*crash my hard drive* (mind)' so I could start again from scratch. I had to stop thinking and start feeling and acting.

Those who have been through it, describe depression in terms that relate to darkness – the black dog, dark winds, the dark night of the soul. Is depression, therefore, the absence of light?

But what is the light?

> "Then spake Jesus again unto them, saying, I am the light of the world: he that followeth me shall not walk in darkness, but shall have the light of life." (John 8:12)

I have heard this quote all my life and, because of my religious up-bringing, I understood it to mean that those who follow Jesus' teachings will live with God, whilst those who do not follow him, will go to Hell. I actually thought it was supposed to be a reference to Heaven and Hell as actual places. However, I now see that this quote takes on a deeper meaning. Was Jesus actually teaching us that those who pursue a spiritually-guided life will have a mind filled with light and peace (Heaven), whilst those who deny their spiritual needs will walk in the darkness of ignorance and, eventually, depression (Hell)?

"The real trick to being in this life, is not to be 'in the know', but to be 'in the mystery'." [71]

Life is a mystery—why are we here, are we alone, what is our purpose?

Illness is a mystery—why am I sick, what should I do, what do I need to learn?

We have become focussed on *knowing* the who, what, why, where, and how of everything. And whilst knowledge is important, we have forgotten that resting in the mystery of things is just as important. The striving for knowledge can become the struggle for control, and control leaves us stressed, rigid and unlearning. If we can find a way to stay with the confusion of the mystery, then we allow *acceptance* to appear. And, it is in acceptance that we can breathe and wait...and learn.

When the space in my mind is filled with light then I am well. When the space turns black then..... I feel as if I am perched on the edge of a black vortex which sucks me in. The dark winds spin uncontrollably and it is so hard to resist them. I feel them pulling my mind in with great strength and it would be easy to let them take me. Easy to let go and be drawn into the vortex where time, space and light are absent. The battle immobilises me.

I do not think but my thoughts spin out of control.

I feel immobilised but my emotions spin around me unrestrained.

I want to give in, to stop fighting and let the blackness take me— it would be easy—but I am reminded that the divine exists in my children. My children who need me and love me. My children whom I would die for.....and for whom I will live. For them I keep struggling against the black winds of depression.

When I read these words, I feel a surge of terror in remembering the pain I experienced, but it also reminds me how important it is to have something to hang on to. Just watching the angelic faces of my children as they slept was my anchor. Knowing that they needed me to keep going, that they deserved my best efforts, that they loved me and are God's gift of love to me. Everyone needs a light at the end of the tunnel to focus on.

I have come to understand that the ultimate source of our mental, emotional, and physical difficulties can often be sourced to our belief in the illusion of separation from our divinity. We are spiritual beings having a human experience. When we forget, or deny this truth, all manner of discord befalls us because we lose the ability to see the divinity in ourselves, and in others.

"An emotion usually represents an amplified and energized thought pattern and, because of its often overpowering energetic charge, it is not easy initially to stay present enough to be able to watch it. It wants to take you over, and it usually succeeds—unless there is enough presence in you. If you are pulled into unconscious identification with the emotion through lack of presence, which is normal, the emotion temporarily becomes 'you'. Often a vicious circle builds up between your thinking and the emotion: they feed each other. The thought pattern creates a magnified reflection of itself in the form of an emotion, and the vibrational frequency of the emotion keeps feeding the original thought pattern. By dwelling mentally on the situation, event, or person that is the perceived cause of the emotion, the thought feeds energy to the emotion, which in turn energizes the thought pattern, and so on." [72]

It strikes me that children and depression represent two ends of the continuum in regards to the relationship between thoughts and emotion. On one end, when I experience depression, every emotion becomes amplified by the 'unbalanced' thought processes I go through, which then amplifies the original emotion, and my thoughts go further out of balance, and on and on. So if we look at how I used to react during those long night-time feeding sessions with my baby, the cycle would look something like this: feeling tired (emotion) – how long have we been up? (thought) – look at the time and feel panicky (emotion) – this feed is taking so long, I'll not get enough sleep (thought) – overwhelm (emotion) – why do our feeds take so long? Am I doing something wrong? Why am I so bad at everything, even breastfeeding? (thought) – sadness (emotion) ...and on and on it goes.

Children, on the other hand, don't engage the negative thought processes in the same way as adults. When my son gets angry, he will stamp his feet and yell that no-one understands. But if left alone, he recovers within a minute or so and resumes playing. He can return to his happy state so easily because he doesn't engage the thought-emotion cycle.

"To some people, surrender may have negative connotations, implying defeat, giving up, failing to rise to the challenges of life, becoming lethargic, and so on. True surrender, however, is something entirely different. It does not mean to passively put up with whatever situation you find yourself in and to do nothing about it. Nor does it mean to cease making plans or initiating positive action.

Surrender is the simple but profound wisdom of *yielding to* rather than *opposing* the flow of life. The only place where you can experience the flow of life is the Now, so to surrender is to accept the present moment unconditionally and without reservation." [73]

Non-surrender hardens "not only your psychological form but also your physical form – your body – becomes hard and rigid through resistance. Tension arises in different parts of the body, and the body as a whole contracts. The free flow of life energy through the body, which is essential for its healthy functioning, is greatly restricted. Bodywork and certain forms of physical therapy can be helpful in restoring this flow, but unless you practice surrender in your everyday life, those things can only give temporary symptom relief since the cause – the resistance pattern – has not been dissolved." [74]

About 8 months after the postnatal depression started, I was in chronic pain with back problems. Constant physiotherapy was doing very little to help and I had been referred to a back surgeon to discuss options. Whilst waiting for the surgeon's appointment (it was months away!) I decided to see if acupuncture could help – and it did! Although I was still in a lot of pain, I cancelled the surgeon's appointment and continued with acupuncture. The improvement to my back was good but had plateaued when my acupuncturist referred me to a counsellor to help with my emotional state. Those sessions with him were invaluable to my emotional health but, somewhere along the line, my back improved too. The process of releasing painful emotions from my past seemed to release the pain. I still have the same anatomical issues in my back; however, I have found that emotional surrender is as important as my Pilates classes in maintaining spinal health.

Lama Surya Das retells a teaching tale that I think highlights a common attitude to receiving help. [75]

"Every summer there is a rainy season; some years there are huge monsoons that flood the Ganges. When that happens, whole towns go under water. Houses float dangerously down the street and there is a great loss of human and animal life.

One year, a devout Brahmin [spiritual seeker] was in his house when the flood-waters were approaching. The headman of the village came and said, "It's time to leave".

The Brahmin replied, "I trust in God alone. He will take care of me." And he refused to leave.

The waters got higher and higher. Finally some people came by in boats and asked him to leave. The Brahmin replied, "I trust in God alone. I don't need your boats."

By now, the Brahmin was sitting on the roof of his house. A log came bobbing along downstream with another Brahmin holding on for dear life. The second Brahmin said, "Jump, sir. Join me."

The first Brahmin replied, "I trust in God alone. God will save me."

Then a helicopter with some foreign aid workers came and hovered overhead, offering to drop a line. "Go away," the Brahmin said. "I can't touch your line because you are untouchables. Besides, I trust in God alone. He will save me."

Finally the Brahmin drowned. Shortly thereafter he appeared at the gates of heaven where he met one of the Hindu gods. "I prayed to you," he said. "Why didn't you help me?"

"What do you mean?" the god replied. "I sent you the headman of the village, but you were too arrogant. I sent people in boats, but you were too stubborn. I sent your fellow Brahmin on a log, but you were too foolish. I sent foreign aid workers, but you were too proud. What else could I do?"

The moral of this story is that it's very hard to see divine assistance in person: it is only visible in actions. Often help comes in an unexpected form and we fail to see it as 'help' because we were expecting something or someone in particular.

During the postnatal depression, when I had reached a point of exhaustion and felt I couldn't keep going, I decided to research antidepressants. They seemed to work for other people so maybe they could work for me. I was worried because I react to many substances in opposite ways to most people – I can drink strong coffee and go straight to sleep, evening primrose oil is meant to help skin conditions but actually gives me eczema, and the hormone prescribed to help my hormonal imbalance actually increased the imbalance. Even though this concern was in my mind, I was so exhausted from the depression that I thought it might be worth trying.

I went to the pharmacy with my script for antidepressants three times, and three times I felt as if someone was holding my arm and preventing me from giving the script to the pharmacy staff. Despondent at what I thought was my 'stubbornness' getting in the way of relief, I tearily told my acupuncturist what had happened a few days later. He looked at me, said 'Let's try something different" and from that acupuncture session onwards, I felt a change in me. I just KNEW I didn't need the antidepressants and I just KNEW the depression would end. I just had to believe in my instincts and follow the guidance of Spirit.

I am so thankful that I was able to recognise God's hand holding my arm in the pharmacy. I'm so glad God sent me to my acupuncturist.

I realise now that I am not yet healed. I may still need to go through periods where the dark clouds cover the sky of my mind. For it is only though contact with the darkness that I can create a path to the light. Each time I travel the dark path and discover another piece of the puzzle, I build a longer, wider, stronger path back to sanity. But as I build this road, each paver of knowledge will make it easier to stay on the path....my time in the darkness will eventually diminish as the path becomes the 'ALL'.

THE ENERGY BODY

"We stand at the threshold of a new era in medicine and healing. Today, instead of looking at the human body as a biological machine, we know it is a vast energetic network, where spirit, matter, and power intersect." [76]

Throughout history and across all cultures, there have been individuals who could perceive these energetic networks that science is, only now, accepting as real. Shamans, spiritual healers, and intuitives have been able to see and work with the three systems that link our physical and spiritual energies, and which interact to form our energetic anatomy. These systems are:

> ➢ The meridians – channels which distribute energy throughout the body,
> ➢ The chakras – energy receptors, and
> ➢ The fields – expanding bubbles found outside of our body.

"These fields compose our energetic boundaries. They listen to the data in our chakras and other energy centres to determine which information to bring from outside to inside of us. The fields also communicate messages from us to the outer world...Our energetic fields respond to trauma and healing energies. They also react to emotions and love..." [77]

When I was younger, my mother used to worry about me saying that I was taking my clients' and friends' problems 'home with me'. Back then I didn't understand this, as I knew that I wasn't thinking about these problems when I was by myself. Over the years I have gradually and painfully learnt that I wasn't taking other peoples' problems home *consciously* but I was taking them home *energetically*. I say painfully because it was only by feeling the negative impact of this behaviour on my health that I learned about energetic boundaries. I am finally becoming more tuned-in and starting to recognise when I am sending too much of my energy out to others or when their energy is coming home in my energy fields. I feel it is important for sensitive people to understand how to maintain healthy energetic boundaries in order to support their health.

In her book "Energetic Boundaries – How to stay Connected and Protected in Work, Love and Life", Cyndi Dale [78] lists some of the symptoms of energetic-boundary issues, including:

> ➤ Feeling overwhelmed by everyone else's feelings, moods, needs, problems, negativity, and even illnesses
> ➤ Habitual people pleasing, usually to your own detriment
> ➤ Sudden, awful attacks of negativity
> ➤ Exhaustion, anger, and frustration from carrying, and caring about, everyone else while receiving nothing in return
> ➤ Recurring monetary, relationship, and work woes
> ➤ Depressing heaviness and physical illnesses, results of absorbing external energies
> ➤ Fear and distraction caused by intrusive psychic or supernatural events or energies
> ➤ Generalized anxiety, the product of always needing to watch for unseen dangers
> ➤ Constant compulsions, which are often signs of tending to others' energies and needs instead of our own
> ➤ The embarrassment of behaving in ways that don't reflect your real self and that allow you to put up with the ridiculous from others
> ➤ The nagging feeling that the universe or the Divine is present for anyone but *you*.

Every human being, both male and female, has seven specific energy centres in their bodies known as chakras. These are said to resemble whirling vortices of subtle energies which are vertically aligned, running from the base of the spine to the crown of the head.

"The chakras are somehow involved in taking in higher energies and transmuting them to a utilizable form within the human structure....From a physiologic standpoint, the chakras appear to be involved with the flow of higher energies via specific subtle energetic channels into the cellular structure of the physical body. At one level, they seem to function as energy transformers, stepping down energy of one form and frequency to a lower level energy. This energy is, in turn, translated into hormonal, physiologic, and ultimately cellular changes throughout the body." [79]

"Each of the seven major chakras has its particular emotional and spiritual lesson to be learned. The chakras connect the organs, glands, and nervous centres of the body with the vital forces which animate the physical body. The degree to which an individual is successful in dealing with the particular lessons inherent in each chakra will determine the amount of subtle-energy flow which can move into the body to maintain proper health. When a chakra is functioning abnormally because of improper attitudes, old self-deprecating message tapes, fears, and guilt, the organs which receive vital flow from that chakra become affected. Total avoidance of a particular lesson can result in blockage of the chakra and inadequate vital flow to the associated organs." [80]

As quantum science is confirming, our perceptions create our biology. This has a direct effect on the health of our chakras, as negative perceptions can create disharmony in our bodies, causing imbalances in our chakras. Because inner emotional balance is partly a function of properly working chakras, an understanding of the chakras will provide explanations as to how different emotional states can create either illness or wellness.

Over the following pages, I will draw on the work of Dr Christiane Northrup (*Women's Bodies Women's Wisdom*)[81], Dr Richard Gerber (*Vibrational Medicine*)[82], Candice Covington (*Essential Oils in Spiritual Practice*)[83], and Barbara Ann Brennan (*Hands of Light*)[84] to describe the function of each of these chakras, as well as how this relates to health, and disease.

Base Or Root Chakra

The base or root chakra is located near the coccyx. Lessons of the base chakra are related to the material world and our will to live in physical reality. This chakra reflects the degree to which we feel connected to the earth or are grounded in our activities.

"The first chakra area is affected by how secure and safe we feel in the world and how well we can balance trust versus mistrust, independence versus dependence and standing alone versus belonging to groups. This area is also affected by the balance we strike between feeling fearless and allowing ourselves to feel our fear fully." [85]

On a physical level the base chakra is associated with the sacrum, the spine in general and external orifices of excretion such as the rectum, the anus, and urethra. These structures are associated symbolically with the process of release. Imbalances in this chakra may manifest as chronic low back pain, sciatica, varicose veins, or rectal tumours/cancer.

The cosmic creative energies which emanate from the root chakra can be funnelled either into procreation (the birthing of new life) or artistic creativity via the generation of new thoughts, ideas, and inventions.

The base chakra reflects the colour red and responds to crystals like garnet, ruby, and red jasper, as well essential oils such as arborvitae, vetiver, myrrh, and patchouli.

Sacral Chakra

The sacral chakra is located either just below the umbilicus or near the spleen. Lessons of the sacral chakra are related to sexuality, emotions, relationships, and creativity. This chakra is motivated by pleasure and is the driving force for enjoyment of life through the senses ie taste, touch, smell, vision or hearing. It allows us to 'feel' the world both inside and outside of our body and helps us to develop our identity via our relationships.

On a physical level the sacral chakra is associated with the gonads, reproductive organs, urinary bladder, large and small intestines, hip area, appendix, and lumbar vertebrae.

Imbalances in the sacral chakra may manifest physically as colitis, irritable bowel syndromes, bladder tumours, malabsorption diseases of the small intestine, various types of sexual dysfunction, prostatitis, arthritis and low back pains, and are activated by a fear of losing control.

The sacral chakra reflects the orange colour vibrations and responds to crystals like carnelian, citrine, orange calcite, and fire opal as well as essential oils such as cardamom, jasmine, rose, and neroli.

"At an esoteric level, dysfunction in the lower two chakras may be symbolic of holding onto old outdated thoughts and program tapes – a so-called inability to release the past. Diseases affecting the colon, rectum, and anal sphincter may be manifestations of dysfunction in the lower two chakras which are symbolized by problems relating to the release of old 'garbage'. Whereas constipation would represent a disorder in which release of old issues is difficult, diarrhoea-associated disorders might be more reflective of 'dumping' and rejection without assimilation (usually due to fear)." [86]

Solar Plexus Chakra

The solar plexus chakra lies in the upper middle abdomen below the tip of the sternum. Lessons of the solar plexus chakra are related to ego, personality and self esteem.

The solar-plexus chakra supplies nutritive subtle energy to most of the major organs of digestion and purification. It is associated with the stomach, pancreas, liver, gall bladder, spleen, adrenal glands, lumbar vertebrae, and the general digestive system.

Illnesses that originate here are related to issues of self-responsibility, self-esteem, fear of rejection, and an oversensitivity to criticism, and include arthritis, gastric/duodenal ulcers, diabetes, indigestion, anorexia/bulimia, liver or adrenal dysfunctions.

"Domination, anger, and abuse of others can also be associated with abnormal function of the solar-plexus centre. Oftentimes this anger is an expression of an inner feeling of powerlessness that may be discharged towards innocent bystanders, co-workers, or even the children of individuals who have too much unvented energy in the solar-plexus or 'adrenal' centre." [87]

The solar plexus chakra reflects the yellow colour vibrations and responds to crystals like amber, sunstone, and citrine, as well as essential oils such as black pepper, cardamom, lemon, and vetiver

Heart Chakra

The heart chakra can be found in the mid-sternal region directly over the heart and thymus gland. Lessons of the heart chakra are related to love, forgiveness and compassion. The heart chakra is affected by one's ability to feel love towards self, as well as towards others in daily relationships.

On a physical level the heart chakra is associated with the heart and circulatory system, ribs, breasts, thymus gland, lungs, shoulders, arms, hands, oesophagus and diaphragm.

"At a symbolic level, the circulation of blood is metaphysically tied to the circulation of love towards oneself, and between self and others. The heart chakra, and the organs it supplies subtle energy to, are strongly affected by the love nature of the individual. When there are negative self-images and self-messages that are unconsciously being replayed by an individual's biocomputer memory banks, the internal image of self and the balance and openness of the heart chakra are affected. Because the heart chakra has an energy link to the thymus gland, and thus the immune system, the psycho-spiritual elements of self and self-love are intimately tied into the cellular expression and maintenance of bodily self integrity.

When there are unconscious emotional conflicts that negatively affect the heart chakra, as in states of depression and bereavement, there is an associated immunosuppression which causes a greater susceptibility to disease of any kind. When the immune system is suppressed by emotional stress and the personality is overwhelmed by feelings of helplessness and hopelessness, the body becomes more open to attack from viruses, bacteria, and even cancer cells." [88]

Dysfunction in the heart chakra may manifest as congestive heart failure, heart attack, and stroke.

The heart chakra reflects the green colour vibrations and responds to crystals like amazonite, chrysocolla, emerald, and rose quartz, as well as essential oils such as neroli, geranium, ylang ylang, and rose.

Throat Chakra

The throat chakra is situated in the neck near the Adam's apple. Lessons of the throat chakra are related to will, self-expression and following one's dreams. "Difficulties in self-expression may be seen here as a problem in exerting the will to communicate one's true inner feelings. The will activity of the throat chakra can also affect an individual's ability to consciously recognize his or her own needs." [89]

On a physical level the throat chakra has influence over the major glands and structures of the neck region, including the thyroid and parathyroid glands, throat, mouth, teeth and gums, vocal cords, trachea, and cervical (neck) vertebrae.

Blockages in the throat chakra may occur in people who do not express themselves creatively. Examples of disease include – laryngitis, thyroiditis, mouth ulcers, gum difficulties, temporomandibular joint problems, scoliosis, parathyroid gland tumours, and cancer of the larynx.

The throat chakra reflects the turquoise colour vibrations and responds to crystals like angelite, aquamarine, blue lace agate, and lapis lazuli, as well as essential oils such as frankincense, lavender, and birch.

Third Eye Chakra

The third eye chakra, also known as the brow chakra, is located in the mid-forehead, slightly above the bridge of the nose. Lessons of the third eye chakra are related to mind, intuition, insight, and wisdom. It is also referred to as the seat of intuition.

"The brow chakra is one of the psychic centres that is gradually developed by various types of meditative practices. An individual who has a highly developed third-eye chakra has the ability to 'see within', an aspect of consciousness also related to introspection. This type of third-eye vision is an inward focusing of awareness which results in clearer insights and new perspectives on the higher causes of both outer and inner world events." [90]

On a physical level the third eye chakra is associated with the brain, pineal gland, pituitary gland, spinal cord, eyes, ears, nose and sinuses.

Diseases caused by dysfunction of the brow chakra may be caused by an individual's not wanting to see something which is important to their soul growth. Energy blockages at this level can manifest physically as sinus problems, blindness/deafness, brain tumours, neurological disturbances, learning disabilities, seizures, and major endocrine imbalances.

The third eye chakra reflects the indigo colour vibrations and responds to crystals like amethyst, charoite, sodalite, and lapis lazuli, as well as essential oils such as jasmine, lemon, and sandalwood.

Crown Chakra

The crown chakra is located on the top of the head. Lessons of the crown chakra are related to spirituality. "..the crown or seventh chakra, which is considered one of the highest vibrational centres in the subtle body, is associated with deep inner searching: the so-called spiritual quest. This chakra is most active when individuals are involved in religious and spiritual quests for the meaning of life and in the inner search for their origins as conscious evolving beings. The opening of the crown chakra allows one to enter into the highest states of consciousness." [91]

On a physical level the crown chakra is tied to the activity of the cerebral cortex and general nervous system functioning, influences the synchronisation between the left and right hemispheres of the brain, and is linked with the pineal gland

Abnormalities in energy flow at the level of the crown chakra may manifest as various types of cerebral dysfunction, including psychosis, as well as physical dysfunctions such as paralysis, bone cancer, and multiple sclerosis.

The crown chakra reflects the violet colour vibrations and responds to crystals like clear quartz, diamond, moonstone, amethyst, and sapphire, as well as essential oils such as lime, rose helichrysum, and melissa.

"Many illnesses which are manifestations of chakra imbalances are the results of faulty data on old memory tapes which have been recorded and programmed into the unconscious mind during early portions of the individual's life...Regardless of their inappropriate content, these inner tapes are used as reference material by the unconscious mind to formulate each person's physical self-image and sense of self-worth. In order to change the blockages and imbalances in the chakras, it is necessary to recognize the bad messages we may be sending ourselves and to change the inner programming. One of the most powerful yet simple methods by which this can be accomplished is through the use of conscious verbal affirmations. By repeating the affirmations of positivity over and over, the destructive inner tapes which contain messages of inadequacy, fear and guilt are erased and reprogrammed with new messages of security, self-assuredness, and self-worth." [92]

Much of the faulty data that is recorded in our subconscious mind came from our own and other people's fears and limitations – 'that comment was stupid', 'your dress looks silly', 'your opinion is dumb' – which get stuck in the subconscious and replay over and over. Affirmations are new recordings designed to replace the faulty data.

Depression is not just *being really sad*. Depression can be the result of unrecognised pain and we often feel angry when we go unrecognised. But, especially in relation to postnatal depression, how can I feel angry when I have two gorgeous and healthy babies, a loving husband, a nice home, etc. What sort of person am I to be angry when I have so much? But the anger is an expression of our lack of power in the face of the illness – not anger at our life.

"When there are negative self-images and self-messages that are unconsciously being replayed by an individual's biocomputer memory banks, the internal image of self and the balance and openness of the heart chakra are affected. Because the heart chakra has an energy link to the thymus gland, and thus the immune system, the psychospiritual elements of self and self-love are intimately tied into the cellular expression and maintenance of bodily self integrity." [93]

Through research and mindfulness I am slowly becoming more aware of the energetic exchange between people and how that affects me.

I find it so hard when people tell me they are not angry/frustrated/annoyed and yet I feel like I've been energetically *hit* in the chest. I feel the sudden drain of energy – it starts in my heart and solar plexus chakras and then I feel it in my head. I am initially filled with anger and frustration at their inability to see how their behaviour and words are perceived. Then as the anger dissipates, I am left feeling sick – churning stomach, shaky, and my brain just shuts down. I am drained.

I realise that the anger keeps me going and keeps my energy high enough to talk to the other person. Without the anger, I am left to drain away from the energetic exchange. I feel like a balloon when the air is let out. I feel like I want to sleep. I feel like I will black out from the energy draining. I still need to learn to maintain my energetic boundaries so that my response can remain calm, rather than feeling buffeted around and using my anger to remain alert.

"..many types of illness are caused by the ego's continuous resistance, which creates restrictions and blockages in the flow of energy through the body."[94] Eckhart Tolle discusses how when we are in this contracted ego state we are *devoured* by thinking, and energy can no longer flow through the knots inside us. That was exactly how I felt when I had postnatal depression – like a macrame creation, completely made of knots.

In this contracted ego state energy can't flow easily and in some places, may be unable to flow at all, creating blockages. These show up in our energetic anatomy – the meridians, the chakras, and the energy body – as distortions and blockages, which can then manifest in our physical body as pain or disease.

In this contracted ego state, it is also so much harder to feel our connection with the Divine. That connection is always there, but the more our ego is in control, the harder it is to feel the connection. Being in the present moment – in the Space of Now as Tolle calls it – allows us to detach from ego and creates space for the energy of the Divine to flow through us.

Essential oils have become a part of my mental self-care routine over the past few years. These beautiful and gentle gifts from the earth support me in so many ways - from soothing physical conditions to inspiring spiritual transformation.

Essential oils have the capacity to connect the mind, body and spirit, allowing me to more quickly access a space where I can connect with a greater level of calm.

As vibrational essences, essential oils are able to resonate with the chakras to help effect balance, encourage clarity, and reinforce courage.

Lavender soothes my frazzled nerves. Juniper Berry supports me to find courage in the face of my fears. Frankincense calms my mind and allows me to hear Spirit.

QUANTUM THEORY – THOUGHT CREATES REALITY

Masaru Emoto has been taking photographs of water crystals for nearly 20 years. Through his work he has shown us that water responds to its environment. Initially, he noticed a difference in the shapes made by water that was from a river as compared to tap water. River water formed beautiful crystals while the crystals formed from tap water was misshapen and distorted.

Emoto then experimented with the written word and music. "Words and phrases that are based on universal truths, such as *thank you* or *love and gratitude* formed lovely, symmetrical hexagons. But water that was exposed to negative words or phrases, such as *you fool* or *war*, produced ugly, misshapen crystals."[95]

If thoughts can affect water in this way, and our bodies are approximately 70% water – what do our thoughts and words do to our bodies?

"As you think different thoughts, your brain circuits fire in corresponding sequences, patterns, and combinations, which then produce levels of mind equal to those thoughts. Once these specific networks of neurons are activated, the brain produces specific chemicals with the exact signature to match those thoughts so that you can feel the way you were just thinking.

Therefore, when you have great thoughts or loving thoughts or joyous thoughts, you produce chemicals that make you feel great or loving or joyful. The same holds true if you have negative, fearful, or impatient thoughts. In a matter of seconds, you begin to feel negative or anxious or impatient."[96]

So, every time you tell yourself 'I can't handle this', or 'I can't cope', or 'I don't know what to do so I must be a terrible mother', then your brain produces the corresponding chemicals to reinforce this. So, then you feel worse. Gradually, this negative state lasts longer and longer until you forget how to feel happy.

We create our reality........quantum physics confirms this.

"The biggest pharmacy you will ever find is the one between your ears. Because every thought you think creates a cascade of biochemical changes in your body that are measurable. And every cell in your body communicates instantly with every other cell in your body." [97]

In the centre of the brain is the hypothalamus. It makes the chemicals that match our emotions. There are chemicals for happiness, sadness, lust, victimisation, frustration, anger, fear, anxiety, etc. There is a different chemical for every single emotion we have. As soon as we experience an emotional state, the hypothalamus produces the corresponding chemical and releases it into the blood stream, thereby flooding every cell in the body.

So, you are what you think—both positively and negatively. Therefore, it is within your thoughts to create wellness through healthy thinking.

"Decades ago, pioneering scientists...had the insight that negative thoughts play a leading role in depression...they found that mood was strongly shaped by thoughts - that it wasn't necessarily events themselves that drove our emotions, but our beliefs about or interpretations of those events." [98]

When I read this I became aware of how much I used the phrase 'I can't ...' during the time I had postnatal depression. I had been saying this every day – 'I can't cope without sleep', 'I can't cope with everybody's opinions', 'I can't handle not knowing what's making my baby cry', 'I can't figure out what to cook for dinner', 'I can't do this on my own', and 'I can't cope with the thoughts in my head'. I'm sure there were many more! And every time I said 'I can't....' I would feel the burden of failure like a heavy weight in my heart.

Then, one day, I heard those words coming out of the mouth of my beautiful four year old daughter. I became aware of how much I was using this phrase and realised that I was teaching my daughter how to give up on herself. I didn't understand the quantum mechanics of thought at this time; I just knew that because she imitated everything I did, I was showing her how to fail. It was a bit of a psychological 'slap on the face'. I immediately started watching my language and reprogramming my negative talk into positive phrases.

It takes effort to change your thoughts – it doesn't just happen the instant you *decide* to change them. You have to remain alert and *hear* them when they start. At first the words 'I can't..' would pop out of my mouth before I realised they were coming and I would then correct myself to say 'Well actually I can....'. Gradually 'I can' became the dominant phrase.

Our children really are our teachers – we just have to listen to what they say!

We are what we think.
All that we are
arises with our thoughts.
With our thoughts
we make our world.
~ Buddha ~
99

"We've been conditioned to believe that the external world is more real than the internal world. This new model of science is just the opposite – it says that what's happening within us will create what's happening outside of us." [100] In other words, our thoughts and emotions create our reality

"Our present condition is not something causeless nor is it something caused by chance. It is something we ourselves have steadily constructed through our series of past decisions and the actions of body, speech and mind that arose from them."[101] As such, we have the opportunity to create a more positive life by choosing more positive thoughts.

"Physiologically we know that nerve cells that 'fire together, wire together'. If you practice something over and over, those nerve cells develop a long-term relationship. Therefore, if you get frustrated/angry on a daily basis, you rewire your brain to develop a long term relationship which we call an identity.

Also we know that nerve cells that don't fire together won't wire together. They lose their long term relationship. Every time we interrupt the thought process that produces a chemical response, those nerve cells are interrupted and break their long term relationship."[102]

This makes so much sense to me. Before postnatal depression, I was a pretty happy person. I enjoyed life and had a positive outlook. I believed in myself and didn't let other people's opinions stop me from doing things I wanted to. When you asked me 'How are you?' I always answered 'Great!'

Since the postnatal depression I find it hard to be happy. I don't think I'm a sour-puss, but I stress and worry more and this keeps my mood low. When I get asked 'How are you?' I answer 'Not bad". I thought I was doing ok because 'ok' felt fabulous after the depression! It hit me one day when my husband commented very lovingly how great it was to see me happy again. I was shocked! It made me realise how different I was.

I realise that years of responding from an extremely stressed emotional state, meant that I had rewired my neuronal relationships. I could accept that as the new *ME*, but it's not how I want to be. So, I need to consciously practice new ways of responding until the neuronal pathways are wired together to reflect that.

Michelle Allan-Ramsay

The thought manifests as the word;

The word manifests as the deed;

The deed develops into habit;

And habit hardens into character;

So watch the thought and its ways with care,

and let it spring from love born out
of concern for all beings...

As the shadow follows the body,

As we think
so we become

~ Buddha ~[103]

True Meaning of Peace.

The most important factor
in maintaining peace within oneself,
in the face of any difficulty,
is one's mental attitude.

If it is distorted by such feelings
as anger, attachment or jealousy,
then even the most comfortable environment
will bring one no peace.

On the other hand,
if one's attitude is generally calm and gentle,
then even a hostile environment
will have little effect
on one's own inner peace.

Since the basic source of peace and happiness
is one's own mental attitude,
it is worthwhile
adopting means to develop it
in a positive way.

H.H. The XIVth Dalai Lama [104]

"There are some very interesting relationships between a mother and a child beyond the physical,. This is very important for us to understand these days, because our conventional science, which is called materialistic science, is based on the physical, material, mechanical world. We look at the body as a machine, and we affect it with drugs and chemistry. But through quantum mechanics—the new physics—we have started to recognize that the invisible energy fields are actually more primary in shaping the material world than the material world is in shaping itself. What we begin to find out is that a mother and child are connected not just by their physical connection, but through energetic connections. If you look at the brain wave of a young child, it's connected and synchronized with the brain activity of the mother. To have the ability to thrive in the world, the child must be connected to the mother, because the mother is the primary linkage for survival.

When a fetus is growing in a mother, many of the fetal cells become stem cells in the mother's system. They found this out when studying liver regeneration in adults. They started looking at some biopsies and found one particular woman whose regenerated liver cells were male liver cells. They discovered that she had a male child and that the stem cells from the fetus became stem cells in the mother which, in turn, were used by the mother in regenerating her own liver. Another study found that many of these fetal stem cells also end up in the brain. What's the relevance of that? The fetal stem cells are receiving the input or imprint from the identity of the fetus. So the mother is not just reading her life, she's also getting signals from her fetus. And significantly, the fetus also gets some stem cells from the mother. So there are cells that are connected between the two and because the cells are the recipients of the identity, the cells are reading the lives of both of these individuals. So a mother is still connected to her child, even after the child has left home. This would explain why mothers, for example, become very acutely aware of something going wrong with their children, even if they're on the other side of the world. When the child is having an experience over here, even the mother over there has an awareness of that experience. Now there's a continuity that we really need to look at." [105]

Science took away a 'mother's instinct', labelled it as 'sentimental' and unreliable, and replaced it with scientifically 'proven' medicine and parenting procedures. Now science is discovering through quantum physics and epigenetics, that a mother is physiologically and energetically connected to her children. Irony?

Epigenetics is a new field of study which has revealed that genes do not determine our biology. Genes are in fact responsive to our PERCEPTION of the environment.

The old medical model treats the body as a mechanism and looks for ways to fix its functioning using drugs. The new biology of perception and epigenetics, says it not the machine that's wrong—it's our perception of the environment that is caustic.

"We are not the genes, we are not the physical body, we are the mind inside the system. The mind via the perceptions control every aspect of our biology, our behaviour and our genes...If we have problems it is almost never about our biology, but rather to do with our beliefs about who we are and our lives on this planet." [106]

Dr Lipton states that there are two fundamental actions that can result from a perception: growth or protection.

Cells cannot be in these two states at the same time. Cells are either in a state of growth (open) or protection (closed). When our cells are in one of these states, then WE are in the same state.

Love is the ultimate growth response, whilst fear is the ultimate protective response. If our perception of the world makes us feel loved and supported, then the blood flow in our bodies is focussed on our belly and organs and this keeps our body in a state of growth and nourishment. If, on the other hand, our perception of the world makes us feel afraid and alone, then blood flow is preferentially sent to the arms and legs, leaving the body in a state of fear and protection.

Fear and stress activate the body's HPA axis which controls the fight or flight response.

What is the HPA axis?

The hypothalamic-pituitary-adrenal axis is a complex set of interactions between the hypothalamus (a part of the brain), the pituitary gland (also part of the brain) and the adrenal or suprarenal glands (at the top of each kidney.) The HPA axis helps regulate things such as your temperature, digestion, immune system, mood, sexuality and energy usage. It's also a major part of the system that controls your reaction to stress, trauma and injury.

The hypothalamus receives information from the environment and interprets whether a growth or protection response is required. When it perceives stress, it sends a message to the pituitary gland.

The pituitary gland sends signals to all the cells of the body to co-ordinate their behaviours. When the pituitary gland receives a 'stress' message from the hypothalamus, it sends signals to the adrenals.

The adrenals produce a number of important hormones. When the adrenals receive a signal from the pituitary advising the body is under stress, it sends out the corresponding hormones to engage the fight or flight response.

What is the fight or flight response?

The fight or flight response is a normal, adaptive response to keep us alive in the face of a threat. Blood flow is preferentially sent to our arms and legs to facilitate fast movement. Our heart rate and blood pressure increases, digestion is slowed, senses are sharpened and energy stores are released. This is the response developed to facilitate our ancestors fighting an enemy or fleeing from a sabre toothed tiger. It was designed to be a short-term response to an immediate threat. Today, our perception of stress is all pervasive and means that many of us are living in a permanent state of fight or flight.

The problem is that our bodies were never meant to exist in a permanent state of threat. When the HPA axis is engaged, our immune systems are shut down. When the HPA axis is engaged, we rely on reflexes; not conscious informed decision-making. The stress hormones released during the fight or flight response causes the blood vessels in our forebrain to constrict, whilst redirecting blood flow to the hind brain to facilitate our reflexes. The forebrain is the conscious part of the brain, while the hind brain is the reflex part. As Dr Lipton [107] says, when we are in stress we are basically "less intelligent" because we are not using our conscious intelligence but simply our reflexive behaviour.

How we talk to ourselves is critical to how depression takes hold. Our self-talk / thoughts are our perceptions of the world and therefore affect our health. When we start to pay attention to our thoughts, we see that much of our self talk is negative and judgemental. We are not very kind to ourselves and would probably never think of speaking to other people in the way that we speak to ourselves. We would have very few friends if we did!

Let me describe a situation I encounter nearly every day and how my thinking changes, depending on my emotional state. Every school day I walk my children into school and pass many other parents doing the same thing. When I am feeling grounded and well rested, I say 'Hi' to other people and smile, I stop and talk with friends, maybe I share a joke with someone, and, when I pass groups of chatting friends, I greet them and maybe join the conversation. I leave the school grounds feeling happy and ready to move on to the next activity of the morning.

On the flip side, when I arrive at school feeling emotionally fragile and scattered, my thoughts are very different. As I walk past a friend and say 'Hi', my thoughts will be wondering why they didn't smile when they said hi... maybe they are angry with me. When I encounter groups of friends talking, I might say a feeble 'Hi' to them but I won't go over and join in. Instead I wonder what they are all talking about and why no-one invites me to join in... maybe they never really liked me and perhaps they think I'm just a bore. When I hear that people are going off to do things together, I wonder why no-one wants to 'play with me'.

The school yard feels scarier to me in this state of mind than it did when I was a child going to school! As a child I didn't analyse every encounter in the same way as I do being an adult. But it is these thoughts that bring my energy down and leave me feeling sad and lonely. How I interpret the same event every day depends on my state of mind and the self-talk that I entertain. If I am unhappy then I perceive the world as threatening. If I am happy then I perceive the world as a safe place to be.

However, happiness is not the problem here, as being either happy or unhappy is inherent to being human. It is our response to unhappiness that is the problem. "If we're feeling okay at the moment, we might see quite clearly that these thoughts are distortions. But when we're depressed, they can seem like the absolute truth."[108]

Attend to your thoughts. Learn to replace negative self-talk with positive affirmations and the more you do this, the less your thoughts will spiral out of control and cause unhappiness to spiral into depression.

The purpose of my book is summed up beautifully by Dr Dispenza, and so I defer to his wisdom.

"We should never wait for science to give us permission to do the uncommon; if we do, then we are turning science into another religion. We should be brave enough to contemplate our lives, do what we thought was "outside the box', and do it repeatedly. When we do that, we are on our way to a greater level of personal power.

True empowerment comes when we start to look deeply at our beliefs. We may find their roots in the conditioning of religion, culture, society, education, family, the media, and even our genes (the latter being imprinted by the sensory experiences of our current lives, as well as untold generations). Then we weigh those old ideas against some new paradigms that may serve us better.

Times are changing. As individuals awaken to a greater reality, we are part of a much larger sea change. Our current systems and models of reality are breaking down, and it is time for something new to emerge. Across the board, our models of politics, economics, religion, science, education, medicine and our relationship with the environment are all showing a different landscape than just ten years ago.

Letting go of the outmoded and embracing the new sounds easy. But as I pointed out in *Evolve Your Brain*, much of what we have learned and experienced has been incorporated into our biological "self", and we wear it like a garment. But we also know that what is true today might not be true tomorrow. Just as we have come to question our perception of atoms as solid pieces of matter, reality and our interaction with it is a progression of ideas and beliefs.

We also know that to leave the familiar life that we have grown accustomed to and waltz into something new is like a salmon swimming upstream: it takes effort – and, frankly, it's uncomfortable. And to top it off, ridicule, marginalization, opposition and denigration from those who cling to what they think they know greet us along the way.

Who, with such an unconventional bent, is willing to meet such adversity in the name of some concept they cannot embrace with their senses, yet which is alive in their minds? How many times in history have individuals who were considered heretics and fools, and thus took the abuse of the unexceptional, emerged as geniuses, saints, or masters?

Will you dare to be an original?"[109]

Sometimes, Spirit calls us to stop and re-assess our lives. I believe postnatal depression was just such a call and by walking a different path to many (ie. without medication), I have been shown new ways of being in this world.

And for that, I am truly grateful!

Conclusion

"No matter what sort of difficulties, how painful experience is, if we lose our hope, that's our real disaster." [110]

I have written this book to inspire hope for this is what will keep you afloat when the storm is raging. It is when we lose hope completely that we give up – the consequences of which can be catastrophic to those we love.

The times that I found the most difficult were those moments when I was alone – when my children were having a nap during the day, or when I was awake during the night after feeding my baby. The silence was deafening and my destructive thoughts were screaming for attention. I wanted a life buoy—someone or something to hang on to. To know I wasn't alone in the storm. I would pick up books, but there were too many words for my scrambled brain. I found chat rooms too negative and besides, I find the internet feeds my anxiety. I found some solace in divination cards because they were just short phrases that my mind could handle and my soul feel comforted by. This is why I have written this book in the format I have. Yes, there are lots of words in the Preface, Introduction, and Conclusion but they are not the essential parts. You don't have to read these sections – the main part of the book stands on its own. It is designed to provide short passages of inspiration that will help you in that very moment you need them. I believe that everything happens for a reason and at the right time. So, when you pick up the book and open it, you will find something that will address your need at that moment. Even if it is just a reminder that others have travelled a similar path to you – and survived.

At the very least, I hope my book gives you comfort during those times when your strength is waning and you feel alone. The loneliness of postnatal depression can be crippling and leave you questioning if things will ever change and how you will go on. No one can stop these feelings but you. Although having people around you can distract you from your pain and hopefully give you someone to share your feelings with, the reality is that depression is a lonely illness. Although others can support you, it is you that must allow healing to happen. No one knows how to heal at first, but just try something. I know it feels easier to give up – the effort to move seems impossible and you feel that nothing will change. But it will....gradually.

I know you want a plan to follow that will return you to health but the journey is different for everyone. There is no magic schedule that will guarantee your recovery. But I believe there are important steps that you can take – in whatever order works for you. Remember, you WILL heal yourself.

I see the journey to health in two stages –

STAGE 1 - *Stop the Downward Spiral*

STAGE 2 - *Healing*

Stage 1 – Stop The Downward Spiral

Breathe: I think the first and most important thing you can do is take a deep breath. When we are depressed we tend to hunch our shoulders forward, which is a protective posture – we are trying to protect our heart from the pain. But in this posture, our breathing is shallow. So, take a deep breath and allow the air to fill your lungs and straighten your shoulders. Allow the breath to fill your body. Take a few deep breaths and then notice how you feel. "There is a wealth of data showing that changes in the rate and depth of breathing produce changes in the quantity and kind of peptides that are released from the brain stem....And since many of these peptides are endorphins, the body's natural opiates, as well as other kinds of pain-relieving substances, you soon achieve a diminution of your pain." [111] In other words, breathing makes you feel better!

Thoughts: Don't let your mind run amuck. The negative thoughts are keeping you in this state. Although the effort to think positive can feel monumental, begin to train your mind by just stopping the negative thoughts. Don't indulge the "I can't" thoughts. As soon as you hear the "I can't" start just stop that thought. Say "I can" even if you don't believe it because, one day, you will believe it. The important thing right now is to stop the self-defeating thoughts before they amplify.

Negative mind chatter feeds the depression. When I was at my sickest, it took too much effort to monitor every thought that raced across my mind. It was during that time that I decided to listen to an audio book because I couldn't focus enough to read anymore. I discovered that I could use the audio books to do the thought monitoring for me. By choosing books carefully, I could play them in my car and the constant exposure to positive thinking started to help me to change my thinking patterns. It's like immersing yourself in water – eventually you get wet!

The problem with depression is that it rewires your brain and the negative patterns become the norm. You actually have to work at retraining your brain into thinking positively again. Audio books are a passive and easy way to flood your mind with the type of thinking that will help you and eventually override the negative thoughts. But choose your books carefully. I find self-help, spiritual, and healing books suit me. Fiction is a nice escape but probably won't help change your thinking. The reference list at the end of this book shows some of the sources that have helped me...and continue to help me.

Acceptance: One of the hardest lessons for me has been to accept that I am not the same person as I was before postnatal depression. I was used to being busy and having a full diary. I started to wonder why I was missing appointments and constantly stressed. Then one day it dawned on me – I'm trying to do too much. I made the decision to schedule only one event/appointment each day. That worked much better!

When my daughter started at school, I had to review my activities again. The school had so many options to be involved in as a parent – working bees, class help, the parent association. I wanted to be involved but just couldn't seem to find the time. I found myself getting anxious because I love being involved and I felt I was letting the school down. I was used to being on committees and projects and it felt terrible to stand aside. But I soon realised this was ok. I wasn't well enough to fulfil commitments to such activities and feel I was doing a good job as Mum. My focus had to be on my family and getting well. Involvement in other activities would present themselves later. My first priority is being there for my children.

Some changes will be difficult for you to accept but it is only through acceptance that you will heal. Getting stuck in the grief for the 'old you' will only prevent you from becoming the 'new you'. And it is the 'new you' that you need to embrace in order to understand the blessings that are in your life.

Stage 2 – Healing

Sleep: It goes without saying that sleep is crucial to healing and in an ideal situation, we would all get enough. Although sleep-deprivation seems to be an expected part of motherhood, this doesn't mean it should go unattended. Where possible, get partners to feed babies during the night, as even being able to sleep through one feed can mean a mother could have 5-6 hours sleep, instead of 2-3 hours. Ask family or friends to come over and look after the children while you have a nap during the day. Even once or twice a week would be beneficial. And try to put sleep before cleaning, sorting washing, or baking cakes. Yes, there are things that have to be done but see if you can leave them until later. I find a 20 minute 'power nap' does me more good than a cup of coffee or folded washing!

Nutrition: I'm not going to give you nutritional advice because there's lots of people out there with more knowledge than I! Besides, there's so much advice available, often conflicting, that it can be difficult to know what to listen to. Seeking the help of a nutritionist, herbalist, or dietician is a great idea if you feel you could benefit from their recommendations.

My advice is this: if you consume something and feel badly afterwards, then stop eating/drinking it. Listen to your body and mind. Food that is not helpful to you will leave its mark – through skin problems, stomach / body pain, changes to disgestion, or by affecting your thinking. You may find your brain 'shutting down' after consuming something, or heart palpitations starting, or hiccups, or constipation. Even 'good' foods cause problems for some people so don't get hung up on popular opinion. Listen to your body, consume in moderation, drink water, and seek help if something needs attention.

Move: Everyone knows that exercise is good for your body and mind. I started dancing when I was 6 years old and danced until just before I fell pregnant for the first time. I never dreamed there would be a time when I couldn't dance. But depression robbed me of the ability to even initiate movement – any movement. Most people with depression will tell you it's hard to even get out of bed. So, forget exercise if it overwhelms you and think about movement. Any movement is a start, and any start is good. Walk around the couch 5 times today and increase it by 1 each day. Walk around the backyard once today and increase it by once each day. Jump on the spot and increase how many jumps you do each day. JUST MOVE. And if moving makes you cry, Great! That means you are moving the depression around and getting it out.

Comparison: Don't compare yourself to others! Comparison starts the '*shoulda, coulda, woulda*'cycle and all that does it make you feel 'less than'. Postnatal depression doesn't make you a bad mum. Not having enough money to buy organic food for your children doesn't make you a bad mum. Having un-ironed clothes doesn't make you a bad mum. Being a working mum or a stay-at-home mum doesn't make you a bad mum. Being skinny, wealthy, pretty, successful, with a gorgeous child doesn't make you a good mum. Just stop comparing yourself, your partner or your children to anyone else – you are all Fabulous!

Reduce Exposure To Negatives: Unfortunately, our society thrives on negativity. The Australian '70's band Skyhooks expressed it perfectly in their song 'Horror Movie' when they wrote 'Horror movie, it's the 6.30 news'. In a half hour news show, you are lucky to get a 2 minute 'feel good' story whilst the rest of the show tells you about all the horrible things happening in the world. Even TV series and soap operas feed this need for horror with explosions, betrayals, theft, conspiracy, and murder. I certainly wouldn't want to live in the neighbourhoods where these shows exist!

The law of attraction means that the more you focus on something, the more of that thing you will attract. So if you focus on how bad you feel, how lonely you feel, how evil the world is etc., then you will make things feel worse

Negativity feeds fear, and fear feeds depression. So, opt out. I stopped watching the news years ago and whilst some people think I'm irresponsible for not being 'up-to-date' with world happenings, I feel better for it. And my children don't need to be programmed into the violence that the media feels we need in our lives. "It's not our job to toughen our children up to face a cruel and heartless world. It's our job to raise children who will make the world a little less cruel and heartless" [112]

Be aware: if something makes you feel negative, then review its place in your life.

Surround Yourself With Positives: In order to change the negative thought processes that hold you in depression, surround yourself with positivity. This can be in the form of feel-good movies, happy music, positive books, supportive people, and healing modalities. Allow others to inspire you to greater happiness. Acupuncture always lifts my spirits and makes me feel like I can move forward in a positive direction. Support groups can be really helpful but don't just join a group because you think it is the right thing to do. I've heard many mothers say they joined this or that group because they thought it would be good for their children, but there is so much gossip and bad attitudes that they and their children come home feeling anxious and grumpy. Better to have played in the park I think!

Remember, the law of attraction I mentioned before? Well, just as focussing on the negatives will attract more negatives into your life, the opposite is also true. If you focus on the positives, then you will attract more positives into your life. Cool huh?

Sing Your Soul's Song: Everyone needs a hobby or interest. Something that makes your soul sing. Feeding such interests is not a selfish pursuit for a parent. Often mothers give up their dreams and hobbies as it feels too selfish to pursue them in the face of family demands. But our children need to see their parents feeding their passions if they are to learn to follow their own dreams.

We teach by example. If we sacrifice our dreams for our children, then they learn to sacrifice their dreams. Do something just for you – sing, dance, weave, garden, paint, write, exercise, bushwalk...whatever makes your heart smile is good for you and your children. Soul work is healing.

And Finally....

Postnatal depression is a multi-dimensional illness that has appeared in your life for a reason. Whilst other people may share their insights and guidance, in the end, it is only YOU that can choose your path to wellness. If you look at this purely as a chemical imbalance, then you may miss the other dimensions of your being that need healing. Remember, you are a mind, a body and Spirit, and the most comprehensive healing occurs when all these aspects are considered

If you take this on as a spiritual quest then remember that you have to be pulled apart in order to be rebuilt. A palace cannot be built on broken foundations. The egoic debris has to be cleared away. There must be space inside you for Spirit. In the silence of the darkness is when you hear Spirit. The dark night of the soul is a journey back to Love. Allow the process to unfold and its treasures will be revealed.

Don't let the darkness engulf you. Allow its lessons and dance back into the Light.

About the Author

Before she had children, Michelle Allan-Ramsay knew she would be a perfect parent! Now that she is a parent, Michelle KNOWS she has no idea! There are no perfect parents – just people trying hard to be the best they can be!

Michelle's career has mainly focussed on working with people with disabilities and she has a Bachelor of Arts (Disability Studies). She has written training programs to prepare her clients to enter employment, as well as programs to successfully learn workplace-specific skills.

Michelle gained her Post Graduate Diploma in Dance and Movement and went on to study a Post Graduate Certificate in Dance Therapy. She conducted a dance therapy group for adults with disabilities.

Michelle is an eternal seeker of Truth. She believes that change is exciting, people are interesting, and kindness matters.

Michelle experienced Postnatal Depression for four years after the birth of her second child, and realised the value of alternative health modalities to mental health. She has personally experienced the gifts that such a journey can bestow in terms of spiritual awareness and connection. She, therefore, writes from personal experience.

Michelle currently lives in the Hinterland behind the Gold Coast in Queensland, Australia. She has two gorgeous children who remind her every day that Angels live amongst us. She is married to a brave soul who continues to walk beside her even though he doesn't know where the path will lead. www.alchemyandlight.com

Bibliography

1. Northrup, C. Dr. *"Antidepressants Discredited Again"*. Accessed August 24, 2011. http://www.drnorthrup.com/healthwisdom/topic_details.php?id=348

2. Dispenza, Joe MD. *Breaking the Habit of Being Yourself. How to Lose Your Mind and Create a New One.* Australia: Hay House, 2012.

3. Myss, Caroline PhD. *Entering the Castle: exploring your mystical experience of God.* Read by Caroline Myss, Carlsbad, USA: Hay House, 2007. eAudiobook. https://catalogue.goldcoast.qld.gov.au/iii/encore/record/C_Rb1046433_Sentering%20the%20castle_Orightresult_U_X7?lang=eng&suite=def

4. Northrup, Christiane. Dr. *Women's Bodies, Women's Wisdom: Creating Physical and Emotional Health and Healing.* (revised & updated), NY: Bantam Books, 2006, eBook, https://ofs-d6030fcaead27cc17af2d7641f32ca8b.read.overdrive.com/?p=nIJPTMTwODNQvQl9P55Dlw

5. Zhao, Xiaolan MD. *Traditional Chinese Medicine for Women: Reflections of the Moon on Water.* London: Virago Press, 2006.

6. Northrup, Christiane. Dr. *Women's Bodies, Women's Wisdom.* Lecture by Dr Christiane Northrup, Carlsbad, USA: Hay House Audio, 2007, Sound Recording, 2 compact discs.

7. National Institute of Neurological Disorders and Stroke. *"Brain Basics: Understanding Sleep"*. Accessed

April 13, 2013. http://www.ninds.nih.gov/disorders/brain_basics/understanding_sleep.htm

8. Gordon, James S. MD. *Unstuck: Your Guide to the Seven-Stage Journey Out of Depression*. London: Penguin Books, 2009.

9. Cabot, Sandra MD. *Help for Depression and Anxiety: How to have a happy and healthy nervous system*. Camden, NSW: WHAS, 2009.

10. Northrup, C. Dr. *"Antidepressants Discredited Again"*. Accessed August 24, 2011. http://www.drnorthrup.com/healthwisdom/topic_details.php?id=348

11. Cabot, Sandra MD. *Help for Depression and Anxiety: How to have a happy and healthy nervous system*. Camden, NSW: WHAS, 2009.

12. Cabot, Sandra MD. *Help for Depression and Anxiety: How to have a happy and healthy nervous system*. Camden, NSW: WHAS, 2009.

13. Ibid.

14. Ibid.

15. Ibid.

16. Ibid.

17. Ibid.

18. Pick, Marcelle., with Genevieve Morgan, *The Core Balance Diet: 4 weeks to Boost Your Metabolism and Lose weight for good*. Carlsbad, CA: Hay House, Inc., 2010.

19. Holmes, Marcy. *"Postpartum depression's silver lining"*. Accessed August 24,2011. http://www.womentowomen.com/emotions-anxiety-mood/postpartum-depression/

20. Northrup, C. Dr. *"Antidepressants Discredited Again"*. Accessed August 24, 2011. http://www.drnorthrup.com/healthwisdom/topic_details.php?id=348

21. Gordon, James S. MD. *Unstuck: Your Guide to the Seven-Stage Journey Out of Depression*. London: Penguin Books, 2009.

22. Lipton, Bruce H. Ph.D. *The Biology of Belief: Unleashing the Power of Consciousness, Matter and Miracles.* Carlsbad, California: Hay House, 2008.

23. Ibid.

24. Lipton, B. H., Ph.D., *The Biology of Belief: Unleashing the Power of Consciousness, Matter and Miracles.* Louisville, Ky: Sounds True, 2006. eAudiobook https://catalogue.goldcoast.qld.gov.au/iii/encore/record/C__Rb1153538__Sthe%20biology%20of%20belief__P0%2C2__Orightresult__U__X7?lang=eng&suite=def

25. Northrup, C. Dr., *The Empowering Women Gift Collection.* Hay House, Inc, 1997. Sound Recording, 4 compact discs.

26. Chödrön, Pema. *Taking the Leap: Freeing Ourselves from Old Habits and Fears,* ed. Sandy Boucher, Mass.: Shambala Publications, Inc., 2009. ebook

27. Lipton, B. H., Ph.D., *The Biology of Belief: Unleashing the Power of Consciousness, Matter and Miracles.* Louisville, Ky: Sounds True, 2006. eAudiobook https://catalogue.goldcoast.qld.gov.au/iii/encore/record/C__Rb1153538__Sthe%20biology%20of%20belief__P0%2C2__Orightresult__U__X7?lang=eng&suite=def

28. Ibid.

29. Tolle, Eckhart, *The Power of Now: a Guide to Spiritual Enlightenment.* Reprint, Novato, California: New World Library, 2004, eBook, https://ofs-c76c34bd102e932b26eb2627fbc135f1.read.overdrive.com/?p=Of5Kh2Q40A3ih32albKbmw

30. Lipton, B. H., Ph.D., *The Biology of Belief: Unleashing the Power of Consciousness, Matter and Miracles.* Louisville, Ky: Sounds True, 2006. eAudiobook https://catalogue.goldcoast.qld.gov.au/iii/encore/record/C__Rb1153538__Sthe%20biology%20of%20belief__P0%2C2__Orightresult__U__X7?lang=eng&suite=def

31. Williams, Mark, John Teasdale, Zindel Segal, and Jon Kabat-Zinn, *The Mindful Way Through Depression: Freeing Yourself from Chronic Unhappiness.* New York: The Guilford Press, 2007, ebook, https://ofs-1d57 04438d3c3605c592ff5096c65218.read.overdrive. com/?p=uWxxky83XhtsWPcHaEUzqQ

32. Tolle, Eckhart, *The Power of Now: a Guide to Spiritual Enlightenment.* Reprint, Novato, California: New World Library, 2004, eBook, https://ofs-c76c34 bd102e932b26eb2627fbc135f1.read.overdrive. com/?p=Of5Kh2Q40A3ih32albKbmw

33. Ibid.

34. Das, Lama Surya. *Letting Go of the Person You Used to Be: Buddhist Lessons on Change, Loss and Spiritual Transformation.* Sydney : Bantam, 2003.

35. Ibid.

36. Williams, Mark, John Teasdale, Zindel Segal, and Jon Kabat-Zinn, *The Mindful Way Through Depression: Freeing Yourself from Chronic Unhappiness.* New York: The Guilford Press, 2007, ebook, https://ofs-1d57 04438d3c3605c592ff5096c65218.read.overdrive. com/?p=uWxxky83XhtsWPcHaEUzqQ

37. Dispenza, Joe. Dr. Accessed April 14, 2013. http://www. healingwiththemasters.com/videos/. (site discontinued)

38. Ibid.

39. Gordon, James S. MD. *Unstuck: Your Guide to the Seven-Stage Journey Out of Depression.* London: Penguin Books, 2009.

40. Williams, Mark, John Teasdale, Zindel Segal, and Jon Kabat-Zinn, *The Mindful Way Through Depression: Freeing Yourself from Chronic Unhappiness.* New York: The Guilford Press, 2007, ebook, https://ofs-1d57 04438d3c3605c592ff5096c65218.read.overdrive. com/?p=uWxxky83XhtsWPcHaEUzqQ

41. Gordon, James S. MD. *Unstuck: Your Guide to the Seven-Stage Journey Out of Depression.* London: Penguin Books, 2009.

42. Mudita Institute. Facebook entry. Accessed January 23, 2013. www.muditainstitute.com (page discontinued)

43. Ruiz, Don Miguel. *The Four Agreements: A Practical Guide to Personal Freedom.* San Rafael, California: Amber-Allen, 2011

44. Das, Lama Surya. *Letting Go of the Person You Used to Be: Buddhist Lessons on Change, Loss and Spiritual Transformation.* Sydney: Bantam, 2003.

45. Das, Lama Surya. *Letting Go of the Person You Used to Be: Buddhist Lessons on Change, Loss and Spiritual Transformation.* Sydney : Bantam, 2003.

46. Zhao, Xiaolan MD. *Traditional Chinese Medicine for Women: Reflections of the Moon on Water.* London: Virago Press, 2006.

47. Gordon, James S. MD. *Unstuck: Your Guide to the Seven-Stage Journey Out of Depression.* London: Penguin Books, 2009.

48. Ibid.

49. Ibid.

50. Ibid.

51. Ibid.

52. Ibid.

53. Ibid.

54. Joy of Living. "Joie De Vivre". Accessed September 9, 2011 www.joyofliving.com.au

55. Nhat Hanh, Thich. *Mindful Movement – Ten exercises for Well-Being.* California: Parallax Press, 2008. eBook, https://ofs-e4edc77e6b12770a4ac53d407a597094.read. overdrive.com/?p=dRR-YzxqAYn8ML827WU5ag

56. Hall, Jackie. *The Happy Mum Handbook. Free yourself from motherhood stress.* Australia, 2010.

57. Napthali, Sarah, *Buddhism for Mothers: a calm approach to caring for yourself and your children*. NSW: Allen & Unwin, 2003.

58. Newberg, Andrew B., & Waldman, Mark R., *How God changes your Brain: breakthrough findings from a leading neuroscientist*. US: Ballantine Books, 2009.

59. McGrogan, Elisabeth. e-mail message to author, October 11.2012. (2012) private conversation

60. Reynolds, S. & Reynolds, E., *"Mothering and Daughtering"*. Accessed March 26, 2013. http://www.soundstrue.com/store/weeklywisdom?page=single&category=WW&episode=7587

61. Chödrön, P., *"How We Get Hooked and How We Get Unhooked"*. Accessed March 1, 2003. http://www.lionsroar.com/how-we-get-hooked-shenpa-and-how-we-get-unhooked/

62. Mudita Institute. Facebook page. Accessed January 23, 2013. www.facebook.com/muditainstitute/

63. Das, Lama Surya. *Letting Go of the Person You Used to Be: Buddhist Lessons on Change, Loss and Spiritual Transformation*. Sydney : Bantam, 2003.

64. Das, Lama Surya. *Letting Go of the Person You Used to Be: Buddhist Lessons on Change, Loss and Spiritual Transformation*. Sydney : Bantam, 2003.

65. Tolle, Eckhart, *The Power of Now: a Guide to Spiritual Enlightenment*. Reprint, Novato, California: New World Library, 2004, eBook, https://ofs-c76c34bd102e932b26eb2627fbc135f1.read.overdrive.com/?p=Of5Kh2Q40A3ih32albKbmw

66. Ibid.

67. Ibid.

68. Myss, Caroline PhD. *Energy Anatomy*. Boulder, Co: Sounds True, 1996, eAudiobook. https://ofs-c235869ba096d964cff85512a16472f6.listen.overdrive.com/?p=WQ6xuK1moHEwdzH6LdaPIw

69. Myss, Caroline PhD. *Spiritual Madness. The Necessity of Meeting God in Darkness.* [Audio Recording]. Boulder, Co: Sounds True, 2002, Sound Recording, 2 compact discs.

70. Myss, Caroline PhD. *Entering the Castle: exploring your mystical experience of God.* Read by Caroline Myss, Carlsbad, USA: Hay House, 2007. eAudiobook. https://catalogue.goldcoast.qld.gov.au/iii/encore/ record/C Rb1046433 Sentering%20the%20 castle Orightresult U X7?lang=eng&suite=def

71. Wolf, Fred A. Ph.D. "Chapter 1 - Start". *What the BLEEP Do We Know?* DVD. Directed by William Antz, Betsy Chasse, and Mark Vicente. Los Angeles, CA: Roadside Attractions, 2004

72. Tolle, Eckhart, *The Power of Now: a Guide to Spiritual Enlightenment.* Reprint, Novato, California: New World Library, 2004, eBook, https://ofs-c76c34 bd102e932b26eb2627fbc135f1.read.overdrive. com/?p=Of5Kh2Q40A3ih32albKbmw

73. Tolle, Eckhart, *The Power of Now: a Guide to Spiritual Enlightenment.* Reprint, Novato, California: New World Library, 2004, eBook, https://ofs-c76c34 bd102e932b26eb2627fbc135f1.read.overdrive. com/?p=Of5Kh2Q40A3ih32albKbmw

74. Ibid.

75. Das, Lama Surya. *Letting Go of the Person You Used to Be: Buddhist Lessons on Change, Loss and Spiritual Transformation.* Sydney : Bantam, 2003.

76. Myss, Caroline. *"Energy Anatomy: The Science of Personal Power, Spirituality and Health".* Last accessed August 12, 2016. http://www.myss.com/catalog/energy-anatomy.htm

77. Dale, Cyndi. *Energetic Boundaries: How to Stay Protected and Connected in Work, Love, and Life.* Boulder, Colorado: Sounds True, 2011.

78. Ibid.

79. Gerber, Richard M.D., *Vibrational Medicine: New Choices for Healing Ourselves.* Santa Fe, NM: Bear & Company, 1988.

80. Ibid.

81. Northrup, Christiane Dr. *Women's Bodies, Women's Wisdom. The Complete Guide to Women's Health and Wellbeing.* Great Britain: Judy Piatkus (Publishers) Ltd, 1998.

82. Gerber, Richard M.D. *Vibrational Medicine: New Choices for Healing Ourselves.* Santa Fe, NM: Bear & Company, 1988.

83. Covington, Candice. *Essential Oils in Spiritual Practice. Working with the Chakras, Divine Archetypes, and the Five Great Elements.* Rochester, Vermont: Healing Arts Press, 2017

84. Brennan, Barbara Ann. *Hands of Light: A Guide to Healing Through the Human Energy Field.* New York: Bantam, 1987.

85. Northrup, Christiane Dr. *Women's Bodies, Women's Wisdom. The Complete Guide to Women's Health and Wellbeing.* Great Britain: Judy Piatkus (Publishers) Ltd, 1998.

86. Gerber, Richard M.D. *Vibrational Medicine: New Choices for Healing Ourselves.* Santa Fe, NM: Bear & Company, 1988.

87. Ibid.

88. Ibid.

89. Ibid.

90. Ibid.

91. Gerber, Richard M.D. *Vibrational Medicine: New Choices for Healing Ourselves* published by Inner Traditions International and Bear & Company, ©2001. All rights reserved. http://www.Innertraditions.com Reprinted with permission of publisher.

92. Gerber, Richard M.D. *Vibrational Medicine: New Choices for Healing Ourselves.* Santa Fe, NM: Bear & Company, 1988.

93. Gerber, Richard M.D. *Vibrational Medicine: New Choices for Healing Ourselves.* Santa Fe, NM: Bear & Company, 1988.

94. Tolle, Eckhart, *The Power of Now: a Guide to Spiritual Enlightenment.* Reprint, Novato, California: New World Library, 2004, eBook, https://ofs-c76c34 bd102e932b26eb2627fbc135f1.read.overdrive. com/?p=Of5Kh2Q40A3ih32albKbmw

95. Emoto, Masaru. *Messages from Water and the Universe.* Carlsbad, CA: Hay House, Inc., 2010.

96. Dispenza, Joe MD. *Breaking the Habit of Being Yourself. How to Lose Your Mind and Create a New One.* Australia: Hay House, 2012.

97. Northrup, Christiane. Dr. *Women's Bodies, Women's Wisdom.* Lecture by Dr Christiane Northrup, Carlsbad, USA: Hay House Audio, 2007, Sound Recording, 2 compact discs.

98. Williams, Mark, John Teasdale, Zindel Segal, and Jon Kabat-Zinn, *The Mindful Way Through Depression: Freeing Yourself from Chronic Unhappiness.* New York: The Guilford Press, 2007, ebook, https://ofs-1d57 04438d3c3605c592ff5096c65218.read.overdrive. com/?p=uWxxky83XhtsWPcHaEUzqQ

99. Lord Buddha, *We Are What We Think.* The Very Venerable 9th Khenchen Thrangu Rinpoche. Accessed May 9, 2016. http://www.rinpoche.com/quotes/quote11.htm

100. "Chapter 2 - What is Reality? A Philosophical Question". *What the BLEEP Do We Know?* DVD. Directed by William Antz, Betsy Chasse, and Mark Vicente. Los Angeles, CA: Roadside Attractions, 2004

101. Michie, David. *Buddhism for Busy People: Finding Happiness in an Uncertain World.* Crows Nest, NSW: Allen & Unwin, 2007.

102. Dispenza, Joe Dr. "Chapter 8 - Neurophysics". *What the BLEEP Do We Know?* DVD. Directed by William Antz, Betsy Chasse, and Mark Vicente. Los Angeles, CA: Roadside Attractions, 2004

103. Michie, David. *Buddhism for Busy People: Finding Happiness in an Uncertain World.* Crows Nest, NSW: Allen & Unwin, 2007

104. H. H. The XIVth Dalai Lama. Poster / scroll in author's possession.

105. Lipton, B. H., Ph.D., *Happy Healthy Child: A Holistic Approach.* Interview with Sarah Kamrath. https://www.brucelipton.com/resource/article/happy-healthy-child-holistic-approach

106. Lipton, B. H., Ph.D., *The Biology of Belief: Unleashing the Power of Consciousness, Matter and Miracles.* Louisville, Ky: Sounds True, 2006. eAudiobook https://catalogue.goldcoast.qld.gov.au/iii/encore/record/C__Rb1153538__Sthe%20biology%20of%20belief__P0%2C2__Orightresult__U__X7?lang=eng&suite=def

107. Ibid.

108. Williams, Mark, John Teasdale, Zindel Segal, and Jon Kabat-Zinn, *The Mindful Way Through Depression: Freeing Yourself from Chronic Unhappiness.* New York: The Guilford Press, 2007, ebook, https://ofs-1d57 04438d3c3605c592ff5096c65218.read.overdrive.com/?p=uWxxky83XhtsWPcHaEUzqQ

109. Dispenza, Joe MD, *Breaking the Habit of Being Yourself. How to Lose Your Mind and Create a New One.* Australia: Hay House, 2012.

110. H. H. The XIVth Dalai Lama. The Dalai Lama Foundation Facebook Page. March 11, 2014. https://www.facebook.com/DalaiLamaFoundation/photos/a.10150178597147816.304826.53912657815/10151956005887816/?type=3&theater

111. Pert, Candace B. PhD, *Molecules of Emotion – Why You Feel the Way You Feel*. New York: Scribner, 2003
112. Knost, L R., *"Little Hearts/Gentle Parenting Resources."* Accessed October 14, 2016. http://www.littlehearts books.com/about-the-authorillustrator/

[1] ... ...

[2] Kloosz, J. ... ...

Printed in the United States
By Bookmasters